BER

Antrim Town & Country

Paintings by Paul Holmes & Text by Alastair Smyth

Cottage
Publications

First published by Cottage Publications,
Donaghadee, N. Ireland 1999.
Copyrights Reserved.
© Illustrations by Paul Holmes 1999.
© Text by Alastair Smyth 1999.
All rights reserved.
No part of this book may be reproduced or
stored on any media without the express
written permission of the publishers.
Design & origination in Northern Ireland.
Printed & bound in Singapore.

ISBN 1 900935 12 0

The Author

Author and teacher, Alastair Smyth has long held a deep love for his native Antrim county. His writing includes books ('The Story of Antrim', 'The Uster Quiz Book' and prefaces to Appletree Press' Chimney Corner Trilogy), radio documentaries, dramas and short stories.

At Antrim Grammar School he has served as Head of the English Department and as Senior Teacher. His interest in modern educational technology has brought his students many national and international awards for educational video, multimedia and Internet productions.

Alastair has addressed several educational conferences in Europe and North America and he is a regular speaker at local history gatherings. Chairman of the Heritage Policy Committee for Antrim Borough Council and former chairman of the Antrim & District Historical Society, he has created an extensive Web site for the bicentenary of the 1798 Battle of Antrim; www.antrim.gov.uk/battle/index.html

The Artist

Paul Holmes was born in a rural part of Co. Antrim and still lives there close to Antrim Town.

Abandoning a successful career in Management, he soon began to develop his talent for painting and photography and is now a full-time professional Artist. Specialising in watercolours, Paul draws his inspiration from the diverse images of the Irish countryside both north and south and, having the ability to recognise quickly the making of a good picture, his sketch pad and camera are constant companions.

Knowing from experience the benefit of formal training, he is now involved in teaching others. His talent for communicating his skills, combined with good humour and ready wit, make his art classes attractive for a variety of students.

Paul's work is on display in a number of galleries across Ireland.

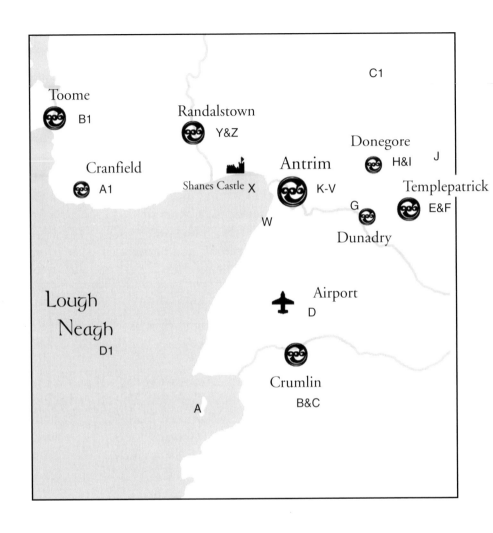

Toome
B1

Randalstown
Y&Z

C1

Donegore
H&I
J

Cranfield
A1

Shanes Castle X

Antrim
K-V

Templepatrick
E&F

W

G

Dunadry

Lough

Neagh

D1

Airport
D

Crumlin
B&C

A

Contents

Beginnings   **3**

Paintings and Stories from about Antrim

A.   Ram's Island - Lough Neagh   8

B.   Crumlin Village   10

C.   Crumlin Glen   12

D.   Belfast International Airport - Aldergrove   14

E.   Templetown Mausoleum - Templepatrick   16

F.   Castle Upton - Templepatrick   18

G.   Clady Cottage - Dunadry   20

H.   Donegore Church   22

I.   Loughanmore - Donegore   24

J.   The Holestone - Parkgate   26

K.   Massereene Golf Club   28

L.   Riverside Mill Race   30

M.   Greenmount   32

N.   Pogue's Entry   34

O.   The Old Courthouse   36

P.   Antrim Castle & Grounds   38

Q.   Antrim Castle Estate   40

R.   Antrim High Street & All Saints Parish Church   42

S.   The Round Tower   44

T.   The Old Workhouse   46

U.   Antrim Loughside & Marina   48

V.   Clotworthy House   50

W.   Reas Wood - Antrim Bay   52

X.   Shane's Castle, Randalstown   54

Y.   Randalstown   56

Z.   Randalstown Viaduct   58

A1.   Cranfield   60

B1.   Toome   62

C1.   Tardree Forest   64

D1.   Lough Neagh   66

The People of Antrim   **69**

Beginnings

Imagine that you are standing on the top of Tardree Mountain about 60 million years ago. All around you stretches a great sparkling white plain of sedimentary rock. The pristine white limestone landscape stretches, remarkably, all the way to Eastern Europe!

Ominous rumblings, initially submarine but later subterranean, begin to be heard. The surface of the earth weakens and cracks. Europe is tearing apart from North America. Molten lava spills, five to ten metres thick, from fissures which open in all directions, running down the hillsides and across the plain between the western Bann valley and the eastern sea.

Slowly, the fiery lava flows cease and begin to solidify to black basalt. White limestone has been submerged. Through long ages more, the land surface begins to weather. Under tropical or warm arid conditions, soils form, wind blown seeds struggle to grow and microscopic forms of life begin to emerge.

Suddenly, all is cast back into the melting pot as the volcanic eruptions return. What primitive life has developed is fried and compressed in an iron-red bed between the original (Lower) outflow and the new (Middle) and seemingly unending deluges of lava.

The steaming lava eventually solidifies to ubiquitous basaltic rock. (The Interbasaltic Bed is distinctly visible in the face of Ladyhill Quarry.)

Under a sub-tropical climate, the weathering process commences again and plants and micro-organisms find an existence on the surface of the Middle Basalt. Then again, a third time, the land fractures. Again, there is a great outwelling of thicker and more viscous blazing lavas, flowing and swirling everywhere, a mile thick, to form another (Upper) layer of the great Antrim plateau. This time, Slemish is probably our main furnace feeder.

The enormous weight of the lavas streaming into the large central area south-west of Antrim accelerates subsidence of the sedimentary Lough Neagh basin. Here, the Lower Basalt has attained its maximum thickness (531 metres). The Interbasaltic bed lies upon it, five hundred metres below the lough surface, with one hundred and forty metres of the Upper Basalt on top of that.

Gradually, vegetation appears but only to drown eventually beneath successive beds of sediments, sands, silts, muds and peat about 350 metres thick.

This process forms what comes, in time, to be called the Lough Neagh Clays, (which man finds useful to work as pottery clay, up to the mid-twentieth century). The skeletons of millions of microscopic diatom creatures create a three feet thick layer of siliceous Bann Clay (which modern man has found workable, about Toome, for making insulating refectory bricks).

Then, (more than 2 million years ago), temperatures plunge as mighty Scandinavian sheets of ice and snow slide in from the north-east to lock everything in an Arctic grip. Next, from Donegal to the north-west, further ice sheets advance, several thousand feet thick. The movement of ice gouges and grinds, rounding and smoothing the Antrim hills of basalt.

Over the central lough basin, the ice decelerates and becomes even thicker as the flow is compressed. As the climate warms, melting ice retreats towards the sea. The saucer-like depression in the vast central plain below us at last begins to swim with the inexpressibly grand Lough Neagh. However, as the ice sheet recedes, it deposits accumulations of rock that block the mouth of the Lower Bann. The volume of water trapped in the lough bowl grows until it can escape through Poyntz Pass to Carlingford Lough.

Retreating ice flows discharge a till and periglacial outwash, which forms the characteristic sands and gravels about Antrim's boggy, fenland lough shores. The final retreat of the European ice sheets (about ten thousand years ago), leaves streams winding round lumpy morainic hills and glacial drift of boulder clay, gravel, shingle and sand. The level of Lough Neagh rises higher than ever. The poundings of the waves along its eastern shore cut into the glacial deposits to form a raised beach cliff. (Lowering of the lough level between 1847 and 1959 has exposed this wide sandy border around the Crumlin area.)

Drainage from the Antrim plateau allows our Sixmilewater, Crumlin and Maine rivers to break out from the hills and carve their valleys down through dense forests to the Lough Neagh basin, while, in turn, the Lower Bann begins its run to the tide. The final touch to the landscape is for the sea to engulf our landbridge with 'mainland' Britain.

Granted extraordinary longevity, we could have chosen no finer vantage point to witness the birth of Antrim than the ancient granite pinnacle of Tardree which survived all unscathed.

Climatic changes about ten millennia ago provided the necessary warmth and rainfall for early Scots Pine woodland to establish itself. This eventually gave way, about seven thousand years ago, to dense forests of large oak and elm, with willow and alder permanently establishing themselves closer to the loughshore. The trees were exceptionally tall and the undergrowth virtually impenetrable. Compact Rush flourished along the shoreline and Reed Mace appeared in the lough's shallow water edges. Extensive boglands were exposed about the Toome area as the lough level fell, (to a water level some three metres higher then than today).

The shallow water, sheltered shore and wet grasslands about the lough have annually attracted 100,000 wintering wildfowl, including Arctic Geese and the wild swans that migrate here from Siberia and Iceland. Springtime ever brings the beautiful spectacle of 750 nesting pairs of Great Crested Grebe. (Sanctuary has been afforded to these feathered visitors ever since the lords O'Neill and Shaftesbury established Antrim Bay as a non-shooting area.)

With rivers, lakes and seas being man's natural means of communications eight or nine thousand years ago, Ireland's first people - simple hunters and fishers - arrived here from north and west Britain in dugout tree trunks, which they navigated up the Lower Bann into Lough Neagh. From this time onwards, man was to be the dominant factor in shaping our local environment.

Our knowledge of the early prehistoric people who inhabited this area relies on examining their megalithic monuments, modern archaeological excavations and the artifacts that they yield. The Antrim district is exceptionally rich in prehistoric remains. From finds of highly polished Neolithic stone axes, we know that the New Stone Age people - who arrived around 3000 B.C. (from the Middle East) - cleared woodland for farmland by ring-barking the trees. Post-holes reveal the location and shape of the timber structures they erected for shelter. With wolves, wild boar and brown bears roaming the thickly forested river valleys, these nomadic farmers opted to live and wander high on our encircling hills. They also found that the land was ready to yield the dark basaltic material that would characterise roads and architecture about Antrim to the present day.

The high Neolithic culture eventually gave way to the artistic and expressive craft-work of Bronze Age peoples (c.1600-500 B.C.) who brought this land to the forefront of western European cultural development. Bronze, however, could not compete against the all-conquering Iron Age swords of the tall Celtic invaders who arrived here in the fifth and fourth centuries B.C.

That an unusually high number of Celtic raths have survived about Antrim can be attributed to a centuries-old local belief in fairies. Anyone who would interfere with the sanctity of these 'fairy forts', (as generations of rural communities religiously respected them), would be certain to invite severe personal misfortune. A rath was also often and misleadingly described as a 'Danes' Fort'; an allusion to the Viking invasions of the ninth and tenth centuries.

Norsemen certainly cast a greedy eye upon the monastic houses that had been established after Saint Patrick's ministry in the fifth century. His teaching of the Latin alphabet enabled his monastic followers to begin recording manuscripts of scriptures, local traditions and history. From monastic records kept in the British Museum, we find that the treasures of Muckamore Abbey fell prey to plundering Vikings.

During the Middle Ages, our history is characterised by battle-hardened Anglo-Normans invading, conquering and settling here, from the twelfth to fourteenth centuries. A more organised pattern of mixed farming became established locally. Donegore and, later, Dunadry became the administrative centre of the 'Antrum' county that they created.

These early residents of Antrim all found that the topography of the area offered natural routes for communications. The valleys of the Maine and Lower Bann stretched north to the Celts' sea terminal at the fort of Dunseverick. South along the Lough Neagh lowlands, their ancient highway ran through Dunadry and Crumlin to the regal hill of Tara. From the east, the Sixmilewater valley led, in turn, both Norman and

Elizabethan English from their Carrickfergus garrisons to Antrim. In the seventeenth century, the route was known as the 'Irish Lonan' highway via Ballyclare and Doagh, which exited the large deerpark of Sir Arthur Chichester at the appropriately named village of Parkgate. To the west, along the northern shore of Lough Neagh, the Bann River frontier could be forded at Toome, giving access to Tyrone and Derry. The lough itself, of course, was ever navigable to all points of central Ulster.

The influx of western Scottish settlers in the seventeenth century left a distinctive legacy in local speech. The Scots dialect and accent quickly established the local identity. Consider this idiomatic snatch of local Ulster-Scots verse: "The blackbird keeks out frae the fog at the broo,/Gees his neb a bit dicht on a stane." There is something economically expressive there, graphically illustrated through translation: the blackbird sneaks a cautious look out from the long grass which is left standing at the field's edge after winter and gives its beak a quick, light flick of a wipe on a stone! Examples of this lasting legacy, affecting spelling and pronunciation, include 'auld' for old, 'frae' for from, 'hae' for have, 'heid' for head, 'ket' for cat, 'mair' for more, 'naw' for no and 'wae' for with.

It was not until the seventeenth and eighteenth centuries that distinctive towns and villages appeared in this area. Four centuries later they still thrive with interest. The expanding residential area of Templepatrick enjoys the distinction of possessing the only seventeenth century castle of the borough to have survived the ravages of the past four centuries. The village's name commemorates the local church and name of the country's patron saint. A great treasure of Crumlin is its attractive riverside walk through a natural wooded glen that, remarkably, contains an old Muslim temple! The quiet, picturesque village of Parkgate nestles amid rural splendour at the foot of the historic Donegore Hill. Then there's Toomebridge, where the country's earliest settlers began the fishing for eels which has characterised the district through thousands of years to the present day. Historic Randalstown offers rare visual delights of a magnificent Tudor-style gateway to the Shane's Castle Estate and majestic arched viaduct spanning the River Maine.

The borough of Antrim, ever enjoying magnificent views over the length and breadth of Lough Neagh, is steeped in stirring history and legend, complete with ancient monuments, ruined and haunted castles and impressive heritage sites. The district boasts a long history of marketing and manufacturing. The area's central location places it valuably within easy access of many tourist attractions as well as convenient motorway access to air and sea ports and the city of Belfast.

The diversity of topography, woodland and habitats about Antrim create a landscape of great contrast and beauty. The soil, generally, of a medium to heavy loam, is suited better for grassland production than arable cultivation. However, along the fertile river valleys, such as the Sixmilewater, the land is ideal for tillage, allowing for more mixed farming. The genial climate brings a comparatively dry average annual rainfall of just thirty three inches, an equitable average winter temperature of thirty-eight degrees and summer average of a warm sixty-four degrees (Fahrenheit).

There have been many who have recorded valuable research concerning the area's antiquities, architecture, church histories, military records, valuation records, literature and industry. Readers seeking finely detailed information on practically every aspect of the borough's past, should find it rewarding to visit the Reference collection at Library Headquarters (Ballymena), the Linenhall Library, Belfast City Library and, of course, both the Public Record Office of Northern Ireland and the Royal Irish Academy, Dublin. To such sources, as well as many local experts both living and deceased, the present writer is deeply indebted.

Ram's Island (anciently called 'Inis Garden') is a picturesque, uninhabited and mysterious Lough Neagh isle, a mile or two south-east of Gartree Point.

Cloaked in trees and hidden among them on the edge of an artificial hill are the remains of an ancient monastic round tower. It is one of the few Irish towers that continue to completely mystify scholars. Perhaps monks of old-Antrim or Muckamore Abbey built the tower as an early warning station to signal when marauding Vikings were emerging from the mouth of the Lower Bann into the lough?

Much of the tower is said to have been wrecked by an invasion of hostile 'mainlanders' in 1121; indeed, perhaps monks chose the site as a refuge from pagan neighbours? That the round tower at Armagh was also wrecked in 1121 (due to a violent storm that year) was, perhaps, just a coincidence?

If ever there was a monastic house here it must have been very small indeed: this tiny island owes much of its present land surface to several lowerings of the lough level in modern times.

An earlier invasion of the island was by Irish pikemen retreating from an attack on Antrim in February, 1642. With what horror they must have watched a fleet of thirteen large English warships - each carrying sixty armed soldiers - set sail from Antrim for Tyrone but divert towards Ram's Island during a sudden storm. A lull in the weather, however, persuaded the English to turn around and return to Antrim.

At the start of the nineteenth century, an old fisherman who owned the island sold it for a hundred guineas. Lord O'Neill bought the property and, during the 1830s, his private steamboat could often be seen crossing the lough from Shane's Castle to his Swiss-cottage summer residence and landscaped 'pleasure grounds' on the island.

The island's final invasion was by the United States 8th Army Air Force, stationed about Langford Lodge during the Second World War. The O'Neill residence was the main casualty.

All its wild folk have now left and the lake isle of Inis Garden has been left to its wild fowl.

Ram's Island

LOUGH NEAGH

A memorable confrontation between a Crumlin man and a man of Carrickfergus origin is re-enacted every year before American television cameras at Chalmette National Historical Battlefield in New Orleans. Though the war they fought has long been forgotten here, the encounter did provide material for a '60s British 'Top Twenty' pop song!

Britain's insistence that American ships bound for Europe must call first at a British port provoked war (1812-14). Crumlin's General Sir Edward Pakenham was appointed commander-in-chief of British troops in America, (in succession to a Rostrevor general who had captured Washington and burned the White House).

The Royal Navy landed Pakenham's troops in the malaria-infested swamps of southern Louisiana. With his men becoming sick and dying in the swamp, Pakenham was forced to advance along the Mississippi to the city of New Orleans.

The well-trained force of British regulars found itself opposed by a ragged band of Americans, Creole Indians and pirates. They were led by General Andrew - 'Old Hickory' - Jackson, (later USA President), whose parents were Carrickfergus emigrants.

On Christmas Eve, 1814, Pakenham's approach to New Orleans came under heavy, sustained fire. The Americans' cannon were larger and better placed, and their rifles much superior to British muskets. Heavy casualties inflicted upon his cavalry arrested the progress of the general from Langford Lodge.

Pakenham's second charge, on New Year's Day, proved even more disastrous. A week later, Pakenham tried a frontal assault on the city. The range of the Kentucky long rifles used by the Americans was so superior that they picked off the British with consummate ease.

As the British broke ranks, Pakenham rode amongst his men, vainly trying to rally them. Finally, Pakenham rode furiously but alone against the enemy and was at once cut down. Seven hundred British cavalrymen had perished; fourteen hundred lay badly wounded. American casualties amounted to just eight dead and thirteen wounded.

Ironically, the British and Americans had already settled their differences, with a peace treaty signed at Ghent in Belgium, on Christmas Eve, 1814!

Crumlin Village

The village of Crumlin was known in former times as 'Camlin', after the 'crooked glen' through which its river winds to reach Lough Neagh.

An unexpected curiosity of Crumlin Glen is a folly known as the Cockle House. Apparently, a landowner once constructed this tiny temple for a Muslim servant, its door considerately positioned to face Mecca.

Silica salts in the river and lough have been famed since the twelfth century for petrifying wood. In times when scythes, knives and gentlemen's razors required sharpening, fossilised holly offered the perfect honing instrument. Peddlers at nineteenth century fairs across Ireland did good business selling such Crumlin pumice stone, crying: "Lough Neagh hones! Lough Neagh hones! Put in sticks and brought out stones!"

Woodland cloaked most of this countryside four centuries ago. Killultagh ('The Wood of Ulster'), one of the great land grants made to English officers in 1603, was assigned to Sir Fulke Conway from North Wales. The property passed to his descendants - Marquises of Hertford - and eventually, in 1870, to Sir Richard Wallace. With rents collected from Crumlin farmers contributing to his fortune, Wallace purchased numerous valuable paintings and objets d'art; bequeathed to the nation as the famous Wallace Collection, housed in London's Hertford House.

The first flour mills in the north of Ireland - built on forty acres at Glenoak in 1765 - greatly stimulated local growing of wheat. By 1883, the small agricultural town of Crumlin was annually exporting thousands of tons of wheat, oats, flour and oatmeal to Manchester and Liverpool.

Glenoak was later developed as the headquarters of the Ulster Woollen Company. The company specialised in advanced techniques of dyeing, carding, spinning, weaving and finishing. The Crumlin River powered its Hercules turbine water-wheel that worked twenty five looms. A 100 horse-power steam engine supplied ample energy for the manufacture of serges, flannels, worsted coatings, friezes, fingering and knitting yarns, and the company's famous 'Lough Neagh Tweeds'.

Crumlin also offers a rare opportunity to admire buzzards, cage birds, falcons, gannet, gulls, kestrels, owls, peafowl, pigeons, guinea pigs, hedgehogs and rabbits. Talnotry Cottage Bird Garden provides a sanctuary for injured and abandoned birds and small mammals.

Crumlin Glen

A sophisticated international airport sits in Antrim's front garden. Aldergrove's main (2,777 metres) and crosswind asphalt runways can easily accommodate the modern world's huge wide-bodied jumbo aircraft.

Britain's pioneering aviator, Harry Ferguson, first took to the skies here in his famous 35 horse-power, eight cylinder monoplane (1910). After the Royal Flying Corps' 1917 training station at Aldergrove had developed into an important RAF aerodrome, the province's first civilian airport at nearby Nutts Corner transferred here in 1963 to create Belfast International Airport.

A veritable new town is constantly evolving at Aldergrove, buzzing with excitement twenty-four hours a day. Ultra-modern airport paraphernalia is everywhere: sophisticated telecommunications networks, security scanners, automatic walkway, networks of computerised visual displays, baggage reclaim conveyor belts, etc.

Aldergrove also invites latter-day Fergusons to learn to pilot aircraft themselves. Alternatively, you can hire a helicopter for a pleasure trip or privately charter an executive jet from Ireland's largest air taxi service.

The weather is a perennial topic of our casual conversation but at Aldergrove, every half hour, they discuss cloud, evaporation, pressure, radiation, rainfall, sunshine, temperature, visibility and windstrength! Meteorological Office observations may provide us with useful forecasts but their principal function must be to support aviation needs.

As well as those serving in the airport's hotel, catering and retail outfits, a variety of mostly unseen people keep the complex functioning properly and safely. Air Traffic Controllers train their eyes not only on the skies but also on essential 'lawnmowing' of the runways' grassy borders. Officers of the airport fire service, always alert for emergencies, also keep runways clear of wild birds; their mobile patrols constantly transmit tapes of distress calls by golden plover, lapwings, seagulls and starlings. Tanker drivers continually refuel thirsty jet aircraft. Personnel of the airfreighting services ensure that handling of airmail is fast and efficient. Department of Agriculture teams keep close watch over the importation of animals and animal products. Customs officers advise that honesty is always the best policy!

Passengers are also pampered with an initial (or parting) glimpse of the province that is the beautiful rolling countryside about Antrim.

Belfast International Airport

Beside the Castle Upton estate in Templepatrick, The National Trust protects an imposing eighteenth century monumental tomb to illustrious Templetown lords; one a general of the Coldstream Guards, another a colonel of the Life Guards and 'Gold Stick in Waiting to H.M. Queen Victoria'. The sombre Robert Adam designed vault - with its leafy swags, circular reliefs and classical urns - is one of the best examples of European neo-classicism surviving in Ireland.

However, perhaps more intriguing figures rest in the old burial ground around the mausoleum.

A few paces in front of the mausoleum's arched doorway rests Josias Welsh, grandson of the famous Scottish Reformer, John Knox, who so admonished Mary, Queen of Scots. When Mary's son, King James I, started enforcing Episcopal church government in Scotland, many Presbyterian Scots and their ministers found refuge and freedom of worship along the Sixmilewater valley. Among the first of the Presbyterian preachers to arrive here, sometime around 1621, was the Reverend Josias Welsh (1598-1634).

Welsh made a great impression on being introduced to the proprietor of Castle Norton (now Castle Upton). The following Sunday, Norton arrived at his own church and ordered the curate down from the pulpit, inviting Welsh to continue the service. Welsh, who spent the rest of his ministry in that pulpit, played a key role in the Great Revival of 1625, following which, the Sixmilewater valley became celebrated as 'the cradle of Irish Presbyterianism'.

Close by sleeps the Presbyterian farmer whose name became the war cry of United Irishmen at the Battle of Antrim. By executing William Orr, the government of the day hoped to teach a sharp lesson to his rebellious brethren in Ulster. It did. Ulster was outraged. Having been falsely accused, unfairly tried and unjustly executed, Orr became a martyr. On June 7th, 1798, Henry Joy McCracken launched the United Irish attack upon Antrim with the cry: "Remember Orr!" Orr's contemporaries were prevented from erecting any memorial and his resting-place remained unmarked until the bicentenary of his death (1997).

Templetown Mausoleum

TEMPLEPATRICK

Templepatrick derives from 'Teampull Patrick', signifying 'The Stone Church of Saint Patrick', built on the site now occupied by the Templetown Mausoleum in the Old Dissenters' Graveyard.

Castle Upton stands where St. Patrick is reputed to have taught during his mission to Ireland in the fifth century. The Castle of the Knights of St. John of Jerusalem occupied the site from the thirteenth century until the Reformation. It was the principal monastic priory of the diocese, controlled by the Ards Preceptory of St. John. This military order of monks - originally known as Hospitallers (after a hospital in Jerusalem dedicated to St. John the Baptist) and now known as the Knights of Malta - served as Knights Templars in King Edward's Crusades in the Holy Lands.

One of Elizabeth I's captains in the Earl of Essex's expedition, Sir Robert Norton, was awarded the Knights' old priory in 1611. He developed the site as Castle Norton before it was sold to fellow captain, Sir Henry Upton. The spirit of one Lady Upton (murdered in an upstairs room with her children) is said to haunt the castle with an icy coldness.

In the early nineteenth century, the First Viscount Templetown engaged Sir John Blore (responsible for the facade of Buckingham Palace) to restore and enlarge Castle Upton. As well as designing the embattled arched gateway to the estate at Templepatrick village, Blore worked on the north wing ballroom, the drawing room's oriel windows and the library's decorated ceiling. As an echo of the original priory's origins, 'Norman' flanker towers formed an appropriate addition to the castle.

Another celebrated designer, Robert Adam, added two rooms, a grand staircase and imposing entrance hall. The north wing and stables, which he also built, remain the most important group of surviving office buildings in Adam's Castle style.

Today, a fabulous assortment of peacocks, deer and Llama-like Guanacos roam the Castle Upton grounds.

Castle Upton
TEMPLEPATRICK

Dunadry (Dun-Eddery) means 'middle fort', sited on the great prehistoric 'road' which linked the ancient Gaelic fort of Tara in the south of Ireland with the north coast promontory fort of Dunseverick.

A bloody battle was fought here in the seventeenth century between Scottish Covenanting royalists and English Cromwellian republicans. The victorious Scots cavalry and infantrymen subsequently advanced on Antrim where, when Cromwellians refused to surrender Antrim Castle, the town was razed to the ground.

In more recent and peaceful times past, however, a happy marriage of agriculture and industry brought prosperity. For long, the district was famed for its rich farmlands of potatoes and oats. Successful local growing of the blue-flowered flax plant (the raw material for linen cloth), combined with the moist climate and generating power of water from the Clady Water and Sixmilewater, made Dunadry an ideal location for commercial linen manufacture in the nineteenth century.

An old mill for paper manufacture and printing already existed at Dunadry. Its proprietor is reputed to have been court printer to William III and to have printed the king's orders for the Battle of the Boyne. With the rapid growth of the flax-spinning industry in the late eighteenth century, Dunadry's mill (like the old paper mills in Antrim and Randalstown) was converted for the manufacture of luxurious linen.

No matter how industrious the mill was, it depended on good communications for transporting its fabric to market. Dunadry's three-arched bridge was constructed in 1832 to carry the novel Antrim to Belfast (A6) mail-coach-road. At the same time, Belfast harbour was developed so that large cargo steamers could ship the linen to Liverpool. Later, the mill even acquired its own railway station.

Eventually, competition in the early twentieth century from other countries, other products and mass production techniques finally ended the production of Irish linen at Dunadry. Though the former mill village has gone, the local luxury hotel features a gallery supported by pillars created from the massive axle mechanism of the mill's beetling machinery.

The old mill-race and thatched Clady House (pre-1780) still impart an attractive country charm to the area.

Clady Cottage
DUNADRY

It was just such a sylvan spot as Donegore that the poet, Gerard Manley Hopkins, described as "a sweet especial rural scene". 'The most Irish' of Irish poets, as W.B. Yeats described Sir Samuel Ferguson (1810-1886), rests in St. John's Donegore churchyard. Ferguson's scholarly translations of the ancient Irish saga manuscripts inspired the great flowering of early twentieth century Irish literary writing.

In his celebrated poem 'Donegore Hill', weaver folk-poet, James Orr, commemorated his rendezvous there with a few thousand other United Irishmen on the eve of the 1798 Battle of Antrim. Comparing work by Orr and Ayrshire's famous Robert Burns, John Hewitt (the late Ulster poet) offered his "honest estimate" that "Orr was the better folk-poet".

Thousands of years earlier, Stone Age people erected a huge fortified encampment on Donegore Hill. Nothing quite like it is known to have existed anywhere else in Ireland. Excavated in the 1980s, it yielded prolific archaeological finds of arrowheads, axes, beads, pottery, flint, food vessels and urns; not a bad spot for such pagan sun worshippers to marvel at glorious sunrise spectacles. Below the hill, they covered a natural basaltic cone with earth to bury their dead. Anglo-Normans developed the mound in the twelfth century to serve as their major motte-castle; a rather good spot for enjoying panoramic views of central Ulster.

From the site where the Normans probably erected their church, soars the graceful spire of St. John's Church, built on the foundations of a seventeenth century church. In its early years, members of the congregation spent the 'intermission' in lengthy services (and longer still after services), sampling ale provided in the adjacent Moat Inn.

Down the years, families took pains not to annoy Donegore's leprechaun community. Neolithic flint arrowheads, locally called 'elfstones', were considered fairies' weaponry for attacking cattle. As the little people, apparently, could disguise themselves as rabbits, a gentle 'earsight' was considered an asset by the citizens of Donegore hamlet. As Samuel Ferguson observed in his poetic masterpiece, the 'Fairy Thorn':

> *They hear the silky footsteps of the silent fairy crowd,*
> *Like a river in the air, gliding round.*

Donegore Church

The eighteenth century marked the arrival of Antrim's first really distinctive buildings: Ballycraigy, Birch Hill, Bush House, Firgrove, Greenmount, Holywell, Loughanmore, Moylinny Cottage, New Lodge, Summer Hill, Spring Farm and The Steeple. Prosperous farmers and linen industrialists invested in creating substantial homes, appropriate in size to their owners' sense of importance.

Few of the tales connected with these palatial homes rival the story of intrigue rumoured about William Chaine of Ballycraigy House, who inherited the prosperous Muckamore bleachworks founded by his grandfather. Across town, his rival, Joseph Reford ran three mills and the Spring Farm bleachgreens which his grandfather had established a century earlier.

Perhaps Chaine knew that Reford was experiencing temporary cash-flow difficulties when he invited Joseph to an evening of card playing at Ballycraigy.

After dinner, the company withdrew to Ballycraigy's grand drawing-room. Among the guests was a stranger whose reputation as a professional card player was not disclosed to Reford. Chaine showed the company to their chairs. The cards were dealt. Chaine appeared relaxed. Reford felt anxious but excited. Bets were laid. Some early hands fell Reford's way and his confidence grew. Slowly, pressure mounted as a succession of games bit into Reford's fortunes.

At last, when Reford was dealt a particularly promising hand, he staked all he possessed. The stranger glanced surreptitiously at a mirror, strategically placed to overlook Reford's chair. Others folded and withdrew from the game. Suddenly, the game was called. Reford left Ballycraigy that night, his entire empire in William Chaine's possession!

Chaine had become the owner of the largest bleachworks in Ireland. Superb gardens, lawns and tennis courts were laid about Ballycraigy House. Fine hunter, carriage and Derby-winning racehorses were added to the stables. Among other residences purchased were Firgrove, Moylena Cottage, New Lodge, Summer Hill and even the Refords' Quaker Meeting-House in Antrim.

Penniless, Joseph Reford was compelled to find employment as an Antrim cabinetmaker's apprentice. Out of compassion for Reford's dilemma, Lord O'Neill offered to bring up his two daughters. Their brother, however, emigrated to found the major and successful Robert Reford Shipping Company of Canada.

Loughanmore
DONEGORE

The Holestone townland near Parkgate village takes its name from a distinctive and mysterious, five feet high megalith. It is a fascinating survival of our prehistoric past. Standing high on an exposed rocky mass beside a quiet country road, the Holestone looks down on impressive views of lush rolling countryside.

The area abounds in prehistoric relics but this enigmatic stone, a relic of the Bronze Age, forms a striking and puzzling landmark that has remained untouched by time across some four millennia. Fortunately, in recent times, during blasting work to clear the surrounding area for farming, the significance of the Holestone was respected.

A cryptically pierced, man-made countersunk four-inch diameter hole, about three feet from the megalith's base, gives the stone its name. We can only speculate as to the original function of such a monument. An obscure tradition holds that the hole will admit only a female hand; this has prompted a custom for lovers to meet at the stone to pledge their undying love. The practice, which has endured since the eighteenth century, is for the lady to reach a hand through the hole for her partner to grasp. The ritual, apparently, protects their union until death.

Whatever its purpose, this ancient Holestone remains the best preserved Bronze Age pillar of its type in the British Isles.

The Holestone gives its name also to a handsome local house, which was built in the middle of the old deerpark created by the Marquis of Donegal in the mid-eighteenth century. Sandstone used in the construction of Holestone House is said to have been specially imported from Scotland.

The Holestone
PARKGATE

Few golf courses enjoy such a scenic setting as the Massereene Golf Club's sandy loughshore 18 hole course (founded 1885). As well as a championship course at Templepatrick, there is also a floodlit golf driving range in Antrim and a 9 hole course at Toomebridge. Parkgate has two indoor bowling greens in a purpose-built stadium.

Sports enthusiasts find endless possibilities here for active recreation. Golf, cricket, rugby, hockey, tennis and football clubs have long thrived in the Antrim area.

Three local rivers offer a feast of game fishing between March and October: the Sixmilewater, Maine and Crumlin rivers. Anglers fish for native brown trout, salmon and the unique Lough Neagh dollaghan. All year round coarse fishing is also available on the Bann and Sixmilewater rivers.

The Sixmilewater has its own marina beside a landscaped camping and touring-caravan park, complete with modern amenities. The loughshore is a mecca for enthusiasts of canoeing, waterskiing, jet skiing, windsurfing, wave boarding, yacht sailing and motor cruising.

The Motor Sports Centre at Nutts Corner boasts a national and European championship racecourse. Top international motorcycle riders are attracted each year to the Ulster Grand Prix road races at Dundrod.

Equestrian centres at Randalstown and Cranfield between them offer a flood-lit sand school, full livery, DIY stables and horseriding lessons.

Since Antrim Forum opened in 1972 as Northern Ireland's first multi-purpose recreation centre, it has attracted international acclaim and been designated a Centre of Excellence for Athletics. There are indoor sports halls, squash courts, fitness studio, swimming pool, tennis courts, bowling green, soccer pitches and a multi-purpose synthetic pitch. Its Caribbean health suite provides a sauna, steam room, sunbeds and hydro-massage bed and a spa pool.

With further sporting facilities offered by major hotels of the area, here is certainly a place where you could never be lost for something to do.

Massereene
Golf Club

From the days of the Celts in the first millennium B.C. to modern times, a common thread characterising local culture was the cultivation of flax and its manufacture into linen. The gold shuttle in the Antrim Borough heraldic shield alludes to the ancient craft of linen making and our more modern textile industries.

The industrial quarter of eighteenth century Antrim town - with its brewery, corn, flour and paper-manufacturing mills - was originally and appropriately known as Mill Row (Riverside). Its paper mill - as at Dunadry and Randalstown - could provide linen bleachers with packing, lapping and ornamenting of their products. Such Sixmilewater riverside mills proved ideal for conversion to house new, linen spinning frame machinery.

The Age of Machinery eventually put paid to the traditional cottage industry of spinning and weaving for selling at local linen markets. With a hundred-horse-power surging down rivers from the Antrim plateau to Lough Neagh, swift technological change in the nineteenth century brought a new landscape of weirs, mill races, extensive bleachgreens and major industrial linen mills.

A particularly advanced operation evolved at the York Street Flax Spinning Company complex at Muckamore. Their flax retting dams were temperature controlled, sprayed automatically and employed hot-air drying machines in inclement weather. An extractor system removed harmful airborne dust from the scutch mill and economically recycled it to feed the boiler house!

Most of the mills' great machinery, which Dickens likened to 'melancholy mad elephants', has long disappeared. Some clusters of former mill workers' homes remain, reminding us, perhaps (as a contemporary folk-poet of the area concluded):

> *Who make the rich? The answer's sure-*
> *It must be the industrious poor.*

Synthetic fibre manufacturing effectively ended the old 'dark Satanic mills'. Uniquely and happily, conversion of the weaving factory in Mill Row's former paper mill has allowed local linen and tea towel manufacturing to survive to the present day.

Riverside
Mill Race

Greenmount House was the setting for a conspiracy in the eighteenth century to destroy the political power of Antrim's aristocratic Massereene family.

Bleach mills on their two hundred acre estate at Greenmount, together with other businesses in Ireland and the West Indies, gave the Thompson family the financial muscle to challenge Antrim Castle.

Though the Antrim electorate paid rent to their Massereene landlord, many weaving families were dependent on the Thompsons for supplies of yarn. The Thompsons decided to stand as Independents at the 1769 parliamentary election.

The Massereenes dismissed their opponents as "a parcel of hot-headed people who call themselves free and independent". Though election success did elude him, Thomas Thompson soon found himself accidentally appointed as legal director of the Massereene estate!

In Paris, the 2nd Earl of Massereene had incurred such debt that he dispatched a Captain John Clarke to take control of his Antrim estate. Clarke duly visited Antrim but, knowing nothing of local affairs, he chose Thomas Thompson to handle the Earl's affairs!

No sooner had Antrim Castle discovered a legal loophole to escape from Thompson's clutches than fresh reports about the eccentric Earl weakened and disgraced the Massereene family. "What his female companions lacked in virtue they certainly made up for in looks", noted the 13th Viscount Massereene. Then the Earl received a twenty-five year prison sentence for a £30,000 fraud!

The Thompsons redoubled their efforts to unseat the Massereenes at the next election. When the Massereenes won (by thirty votes), the Thompsons' appeal against 'unfair influence and bribery' brought some rebuke for the Massereenes but the election outcome stood.

At the final attempt, a Thompson accusation of pre-election bribery against the victorious Massereene was upheld and the contest re-run; when Massereene defeated Thompson by 70 votes to 69, the predictable objection from Thompson was dismissed. The year was 1790. Before the decade was out, the political struggle would be contested by bloody force of arms on Antrim's main street.

Today, as Greenmount Agricultural College (established 1912), an information centre and nature trail seek to promote better public appreciation of good countryside management.

Greenmount

Pogue's Entry found international fame as the setting of one of the best-loved books by an Ulster author, 'My Lady of the Chimney Corner.' The poignant love story of the educated Catholic farm girl from Crumlin and the illiterate Protestant journeyman shoemaker of Antrim is full of laughter and tears.

Anna and Jamie Irvine raised their family in Pogue's mean entry amid grinding poverty. "Poverty inadequately describes the condition of life in that Entry," insisted Alexander Irvine, author of 'My Lady'. "It was stark destitution. We were all chronically, hopelessly hungry and utterly unconscious that there was anything unusual about it."

When Anna told stories of fairies bringing a loaf of bread to feed hungry people, Alexander recalled: "It was always baked in Sam Johnston's bakery. If magic medicine was the subject, it always came from the little shop of the town herbalist, Miss McGreevy. Knights in shining armour were always Massereenes or O'Neills. Our leprechauns and banshees lived in the woods near Lough Neagh or along the banks of the Sixmilewater. Jason's fleet of ships that went in search of the Golden Fleece, sailed south on Lough Neagh from Antrim Bay to Coney Island."

Though Alexander began life as a ragged and unschooled Antrim urchin, he achieved international renown as a remarkable writer, preacher and socialist. He taught himself to read and write, served in the Royal Marines, attended both Oxford and Yale universities, exposed corruption at the highest levels and was a chaplain in Flanders during the Great War. Both the US President and British Prime Minister valued his assistance.

The tiny cabin has been preserved, complete with original mud floor and small half-loft where the family slept like spoons in a drawer. Viscount Massereene requested, in 1934: "that this humble dwelling may be kept intact and unspoiled by time or circumstance, to bear silent and eloquent witness to the great love that dwelt there; and to the affection and reverence that a son of Antrim has for his mother."

To visit the Irvines' cottage today is to stand on a stage on which was played a most human and moving drama.

Speak softly, stranger, whisper here a prayer
For all who toil in darkness and suffer in despair.
Alexander Irvine (1863-1941)

Pogue's Entry

Within a few years of adding a courtroom to Antrim's old Market House, the building became the centre-piece of a major battle, which helped hasten the formation of the United Kingdom.

When Lord O'Neill (Shane's Castle) chose it as the venue for the county's magistrates to discuss the imposition of martial law, United Irishmen plotted to besiege the building and hold the magistrates as hostages. Though O'Neill was fatally wounded in the ensuing Battle of Antrim (June 7th, 1798), Crown forces eventually defeated the rebels.

The old market square and main street had been a popular venue for markets and fairs ever since 1605. The inevitable disputes and assaults of fair days prompted a need for the upper floor of the Market House to serve as a courtroom. In the early eighteenth century, the County Antrim Grand Jury awarded £150 "towards building and carrying on a Session House in the town of Antrim in and for said county". Part of the ground floor served as 'a wretched little cluster of filthy barbarous cells'.

A novel means was found to convert the old rough masonry Market House to a grand Florentine style Courthouse. The new building was built over and around the original, so the historic old Market House survives intact inside the Courthouse! Also surviving is the desperate attempt by a stonemason to correct his spelling gaffe on the Courthouse's 1726 datestone.

It is a wonder anyone ever appeared at the Courthouse's petty sessions during the nineteenth century if the writer of the ordnance survey memoir of the day is to be believed: "The Chief Constable is rarely effective, being most of his time absent or unwell, and might as well be anywhere else as he has no duty to do, or rather does no duty farther than connected with the payment or management of the affairs of his men".

Trespasses, assaults, wage disputes and, occasionally, a mill proprietor facing a charge of smuggling in breach of the revenue laws were the typical business of the petty sessions. For fear of prisoners escaping into the market day crowds, an underground tunnel was dug from the courthouse to the old Victorian police barracks across Market Square.

The Old Courthouse

It is our gain that the Massereene family was never able to modernise their castle grounds. When improving grand estates was in vogue in the early nineteenth century, the Massereenes could not afford to upgrade their old-fashioned seventeenth century demesne.

As a result, the Anglo-Dutch water gardens of Antrim Castle are one of only three such gardens surviving in the British Isles. The long, split-level, twin ornamental canals, sheltered by towering clipped lime and hornbeam hedges, are now unique in Ireland.

One Massereene lord loved to challenge a dinner guest to a walking race along the length of the canals. The guest would be invited to take the path on the eastern side, while Massereene strolled along the opposite bank. On the eastern side, a blind break in the hedging conceals where his lordship had his guest's path detour round a side extension he had added to the lower canal!

The restored parterre garden reveals how geometric design (not colour) was the characteristic feature of such formal gardens. A raised area (with fan-trained apple trees) allows the patterning to be viewed to better effect. Modern horticulturists were sorely tasked to acquire its exceedingly rare seventeenth century culinary and medicinal plants.

About the rhododendrons and flowering shrubs wound a 'Lovers' Progress' trail, featuring introduction wells, pouting arbours and declaration groves but concluding with a divorce pond! Near the Anglo-Norman motte - which the Massereenes dressed with a spiral walk and manicured hedge - a splendid Mexican pine produces the most gigantic of cones.

During the 'Roaring Twenties', Lady Diana Skeffington (daughter of Viscount Massereene) created a stir when word circulated that she was a possible match for Edward, Prince of Wales, (son of George V and Queen Mary). Any chance of the beautiful Lady Diana swopping Antrim Castle for Buckingham Palace melted when the young debutante succumbed to typhoid fever. She sleeps in the small cemetery beside the canals.

Prince Edward became (the uncrowned) King Edward VIII, forced into abdication and retirement later as the Duke of Windsor with his Duchess, Mrs. Wallis Simpson. But what if the young 22-year-old Lady Diana from Antrim had lived?

Antrim Castle & Grounds

Antrim Castle and its beautiful wooded estate seemed an idyllic home for Sir Hugh Clotworthy in the early 1600s.

However, as Sir Hugh's young bride, Lady Marian Clotworthy found life at Antrim Castle a lonely and miserable existence. Her husband was often absent on military business. She pined for the excitement and glamour of her girlhood days at Carrickfergus Castle.

Marian whiled away long hours wandering through the woodlands of the castle grounds. On one of her solitary strolls, she was confronted by a huge, savage wolf. At once, the beast sprang at her. Marian screamed and collapsed in a faint.

Upon awakening, her gaze fell upon an incredible sight. The wolf lay dead, badly savaged. Standing guard by her side was an Irish Wolfhound, itself badly injured. Together, they made their way back to the castle where she tended her protector. It was the beginning of a beautiful friendship. The shaggy guardian escorted Lady Marian on her daily rambles. Their close companionship was set to save many lives.

One stormy night, armed enemies crept stealthily towards the castle. Just as they were about to attack, a wild barking alerted those asleep within the castle. In the midst of fierce firing, an agonised howl - as if from a beast - was heard. The castle was saved but daylight revealed a trail of blood that led to the wolfhound's corpse.

By encasing the hound in stone and mounting it upon one of his castle's front towers, Sir Hugh shrewdly calculated the effigy's potential to ward off hostile but superstitious enemies. As added insurance, he propagated a belief that if ever the statue should be removed, the Massereene family would "speedily decay".

Later alterations to the castle caused the statue to be taken down, initially to a wall of the estate and, subsequently, to its present location on the leisure centre's lawn.

The castle quickly decayed after a fire in 1922 and the Massereene family has removed itself to England.

Antrim Castle Estate

Elizabethan English created Antrim's old High Street between their castle and parish church.

The 1596 datestone of All Saints Parish Church indicates it was only the fourth Anglican church then in Ireland. Originally, however, both Anglican and Presbyterian Scot worshipped here, a practice soon ended during the reign of Charles I. Still visible are some 'Leper Squint' holes, drilled through the church walls (originally for defensive purposes) which enabled God's Word to reach 'undesirables' who were refused entry to the building's interior.

Most undesirable was the visit paid by a Scottish Covenanting army in 1649. Under the command of Major General Robert Munro, church and town were burned to the ground.

The church thatch again went up in flames when rebellion erupted in 1798. The churchyard was commandeered by United Irishmen, while military HQ was set up beside the Market House. High Street became the stage for the famous Battle of Antrim. The local yeomanry captain, Rev. George Macartney (Episcopalian vicar of Antrim and Templepatrick), enjoyed the distinction of being the first official to warn the Irish House of Commons about the impending insurrection of United Irishmen in Ulster.

It was Macartney who added the church's dominant architectural features: the tall tower and lofty spire. The interior is notable for its magnificent open-timber ceiling and sculpted monuments to the lords and earls of Massereene.

John Howe, the celebrated English Puritan preacher and sometime domestic chaplain to Oliver Cromwell, here composed two classic Christian texts: 'The Vanity of this Mortal Life' and 'The Good Man, the Living Temple of God'; for which books, Howe still earns entries in modern biographical dictionaries.

Today, a steady stream of visitors, from North America to South Australia, still calls at the parish churchyard to pay their respects to the humble parents whom Dr. Alexander Irvine immortalised in his classic tale, 'My Lady of the Chimney Corner'.

"How curious that, although many rich and noble people have been buried there during the centuries, only the graves of a cobbler and his wife draw all sorts and conditions of people to that old graveyard," observed Irvine.

High Street & All Saints Parish Church

No-one really knows why or how or when round towers were built. There exists an unkind tale that when Saint Patrick sketched instructions for the construction of a stone-lined holy well, his monks, unfortunately, read the plan upside down!

Antrim's round tower is one of the finest round towers in Ireland. It is the older, taller and more accessible of the only complete pair surviving in the north. It was also the earliest tower to be officially documented: a sketch of c.1699 is held in the British Museum's Lhuyd collection.

A disciple of Saint Patrick founded a monastery here in the late fifth century. Brehon law awarded monasteries the possessions of any stranger dying within the sound of a 'cloc tee' (bell-tower). In this once extensively forested land, perhaps a bell's sound carried farther from the top of such an ecclesiastical belfry?

Traditional opinion holds that piratical Viking raids in the tenth century provoked monks to build these towers as places of refuge. But Vikings never attacked Antrim's tower. Could such an architecturally sophisticated structure have been thrown up in a hurry? Amid hostile pagan clans, the round tower would have offered an impregnable refuge both for the brethren and monastic valuables.

Whatever its purpose, the tower has stood for over a thousand years. Given its construction with lime mortar - a distinctly Roman technique - such building would have been possible any time from the arrival of monks from Western Europe and post-Roman Britain in the seventh century.

At the tower's base sits a gigantic stone with a nine inch deep hollow and a second some three inches deep. That a witch was so annoyed with the erection of the tower she jumped from its summit to leave knee and elbow imprints in this 'Witch's Stone' is a tale which probably originated within our nineteenth century tourist board! Originally sited 120 yards north of the tower, this 'bullaun stone' probably served the old monastery as a kitchen table, grain being ground and washed in its man-made hollows.

The Round Tower

Workhouses were built, to a standard design, across Ireland during the mid-nineteenth century. The neat appearance of Antrim Union Workhouse amid pleasant grounds today belies the dreary place this must have been.

Antrim Workhouse was established on the eve of seven infamous years that were to witness the Great Famine in Ireland. Antrim, however, was comparatively little affected as wage labour insulated the area from the worst effects of bad harvests, a common feature of the agricultural cycle.

The Poor Law included provision for victims of disease. A fierce cholera epidemic had swept through the Antrim area in 1839. Within two or three years, the Workhouse hospital, infirmary and office block opened to provide relief for chronically poor citizens and treatment for fever sufferers. Following a significant outbreak of disease in 1846-47, 'fever sheds' were added in 'Black 47' and quickly became overcrowded.

For those who provided basic relief, as well as the poor themselves, the Workhouse was viewed essentially as a deterrent. It was made deliberately unattractive to minimise numbers seeking relief thereby reducing the burden on local rate payers. It offered only a monotonous diet of rice, soup, bread or oatmeal. There was enforced labour, strict regimentation and segregation according to gender and age.

Whether it was its prohibition of alcohol, tobacco and playing cards or its being seen as the social dustbin, even the miserably destitute viewed it as the last resort of the desperate. Over a thousand little identical boards marked its pauper graveyard at the rear. Some thought it best that, all things considered, they should just die and avoid the workhouse experience.

The War Office requisitioned the Workhouse in 1914 as a military barrack and store. An outbreak of diphtheria during the war forced the fever hospital to reopen. After the war, it became the first workhouse in the north to be converted into a district hospital, functioning successfully as the Massereene Hospital until its closure in the 1990s.

The Old Workhouse

Though five of Ulster's six counties border the greatest freshwater lake in these islands, about half of the Lough Neagh shoreline belongs to Antrim. Where the Sixmilewater reaches the lough is an ideal spot to ramble or participate in a wide range of leisure pursuits and watersports.

From the river's fifty-berth marina, boating enthusiasts embark on cruises of this great inland sea. Unhappily, the first iron lake-steamer in Ireland ran aground (1842), pitching her captain headfirst into the lough. Beside the Massereene golf links, Kay Don rehearsed his 'Miss England 2' for the world water-speed record (1931), which he subsequently set at the River Plate, South America.

Barbecues, carnivals, skiing, dances and sheep-roastings in the middle of the lough were popular during the winter of 1740 when the 153 square miles of the lough froze solid, twenty feet thick in places. During the 'black frost', horsedrawn coaches were driven from the shores of Antrim to Tyrone, Armagh and Derry. Following the great thaw and floods, local people endured a biblical ordeal of prolonged drought followed by fire, famine and plague.

If deep frozen ice was an exception, flooding tended to be a regular occurrence before the lough level was lowered in modern times. An eighteenth century Lord Bishop of Down and Connor complained about land being "entirely drowned, and that a fisherman, having twice removed his habitation, was about to do so again, complaining that he knew not where to set it, for the lough followed him".

Among the most dramatic events on these waters were the Viking invasion of 827 A.D. and a bloody Anglo-Irish naval battle in 1643. Echoes of world war reverberate from the derelict torpedo-testing platform, constructed by the Admiralty in 1942.

There may not be a Lough Neagh monster but there are trout-like dollaghan and pollan (salt-water herring, trapped in the lough after prehistoric sea floods subsided). Pollan was once a popular, tasty and cheap Ulster dish. Eel fishing on the lough has sustained generations from time immemorial.

Since before the dawn of history, light refracted over the great lough has painted evening skies about Antrim with sensational sunsets.

Antrim Loughside & Marina

The combined fortunes of two great noble families were invested in developing Antrim Castle in the early part of the nineteenth century.

Lady Harriett Skeffington, (Viscountess Massereene), had inherited the 'old frowning keep' that was Antrim Castle. When "some of the highest names on the list of the peerage were proud to be enrolled as her suitors," noted the first (and only) Earl O'Neill of Shane's Castle, she chose the second Viscount Ferrard of Dunleer, County Louth.

The Massereene and Ferrard couple at once set about transforming their castle-keep into a superlative mansion and developing a home farm complex. For their grooms and stable lads, they provided Clotworthy House: an elegant Flemish style coach-house with an enclosed exercise yard and stables.

Curiously, though the Massereene and Ferrard motto is 'Per Angusta Ad Augusta' ('through hardships to honour'), above the grand entrance gates of Clotworthy House, the sculpted armorial bearings boast, nonsensically, 'Per Augusta Ad Augusta'!

Flanking the arched gateway are the sculpted heads of a good, God-fearing blind tenant and his ugly wife; a veritable sermon in stone from the master mason. Apparently, the Almighty rewarded the pious man's craving for the gift of sight to behold the stunning beauty of his wife which, hitherto, he could only imagine from her graphic descriptions of herself. However, with his prayer answered, one look at his shrewish wife and the disillusioned husband promptly prayed again- for the restoration of his blindness!

A century later, when fire gutted Antrim Castle in 1922, the Massereene family removed to the Clotworthy coach-house as their official residence. Upon the death of the fifth Viscount Massereene (1956), the family finally left Antrim to reside at Chilham Castle, Canterbury.

Clotworthy House became Northern Ireland's first Community Arts Centre, featuring indoor and outdoor theatres, cinema, museum resource, exhibition galleries and workshops for local craftsmen. It has developed into a noted visual arts exhibition centre with ultra-modern sound and lighting systems and a studio theatre, which can be adapted for presentation of a variety of art forms.

Clotworthy House

Both wet and dry woodlands around Antrim Bay offer peace and tranquillity and special delights for the rambler and botanist. The colourful vegetation of the loughshore comprises more than seven hundred species of flora.

Willow, birch and common alder trees flourish throughout Reas Wood at the edge of Lough Neagh. Dog's Mercury grows in shady woodland spots. Common Yellow Flag covers the marshy areas. Brookweed may be discovered in the damp, sandy parts of the loughshore between Antrim and Shane's Castle.

Several rare species of beautiful wild orchids are to be found, if sparingly distributed. Only among the woods along the lough's Antrim shore can we find the Early Purple Orchid. Scarce too are the Fragrant Orchid, Greater Butterfly Orchid of Shane's Castle estate, the Lesser Butterfly Orchid of the Toome area and the Frog Orchid which favours Killead's grasslands. The very rare Bird's-Nest Orchid and the extremely rare Irish Lady's Tresses (or Drooping Lady's Tresses) American Orchid have each been identified at Crumlin's Lennymore Bay and Shane's Castle estate.

One plant which seems to have adopted the Antrim area as its main home is Wood Meadow-Grass. It particularly favours our dry woodlands and old basalt walls. It has flourished between the Sixmilewater and Maine rivers and for several miles alongside both.

Harder to find, (since the lough level was lowered by recent dredgings of the Lower Bann), are the once common Yellow Loosestrife, bullrushes, reeds and sedges. Where now the Spring Whitlow grass which once cloaked the old wall around Antrim Castle and the gravelly mouths of the Sixmilewater and Crumlin rivers? In the early twentieth century, the Loddon Lily grew on the wet peaty ground between Antrim and Langford Lodge but it now appears to be almost extinct. The designation of Lough Neagh as an Area of Scientific Interest (1968) should offer some protection for our rare flora (and invertebrates).

Looking out across the lough, bird watchers may spy Arctic geese, coots, curlew, the wonderfully named Great-Crested Grebe, heron, jays, lapwing, mallard, sand-pipers, snipe, swans, teal, water-hens and widgeon, (though these will not necessarily appear in alphabetical order!).

Reas Wood
ANTRIM BAY

- Paul Holmes -

Once upon a time, a medieval lord (O'Neill) of Shane's Castle interfered with a fairy-thorn tree. As retribution, the fairies stole his little daughter, Kathleen. Ever since, Kathleen's wailing banshee keen has been reputed to presage some great misfortune about to befall the O'Neills.

Apparently, some castle guests distinctly heard the banshee as they stumbled out of a grand party on the night of May 15th, 1816. That night, fire gutted Shane's Castle. A new castle, built in 1865, stood less than sixty years before it too was destroyed by fire.

However, the O'Neills have long sought comfort from an altogether different kind of tall story. On a lofty tower of the old castle ruins clings an ancient figurehead, known as 'the Black Head'. Tradition holds that only when the effigy falls will the O'Neill dynasty end.

And what a dynasty this is. The Clanaboy (or Clandeboy) O'Neills trace descent from the Holy Roman Emperor Charlemagne, through both Louis XIV of France and Philip of Spain, as well as from the ancient Gaelic Iron Age pagan kings of Tara. With an ancestry authenticated as far back as 360 A.D., the O'Neills form Europe's oldest dynastic family.

The family tree lists numerous notable and tragic figures. One Lord O'Neill was assassinated during the 1798 Battle of Antrim. When the heir of the first Baron O'Neill was killed during World War I, his grandson, Shane, succeeded to the estate but he too died in action while commanding the North Irish Horse during the Second World War. Shane's widow, Anne Charteris, later married Ian Fleming, the 'father' of twentieth century fiction super-hero, James Bond. Shane and Anne's son, Raymond, is the present Lord O'Neill of Shane's Castle.

The Red Hand of O'Neill was adopted both as the Ulster emblem and as the insignia of the order of Baronet by James I. However, on the Massereene shield at Antrim Castle's gatehouse, the red hand is presented erroneously as a left hand! The correct emblem is the O'Neills' uplifted 'Dextri Dei' (Right Hand of God), displayed upon Randalstown's flamboyant Tudor-style gateway to the Shane's Castle estate.

Shane's Castle
RANDALSTOWN

Who Randal was and how a town was named after him is a curious tale. From his great grandfather, (the legendary North Antrim chieftain, Sorley Boy Macdonnell), he had inherited territory across north-east Antrim. The bleak peninsular fortress of Dunluce was his ancestral home.

When young Randal cast his eye over English court circles in search of a bride, his choice of Lady Rose O'Neill must have raised a few eyebrows around North Antrim. Her grandfather, Shane O'Neill, had once attacked Dunluce Castle and taken Sorley Boy prisoner. Shortly after, when the Macdonnells threw a banquet for their traditional O'Neill enemy, they murdered Shane and rescued Sorley Boy.

Rose O'Neill had been lady-in-waiting to Princess Mary, daughter of Charles I. Subsequently, she is reputed to have acted as nanny to young prince William (who later was crowned as England's King William III).

Lady Rose inherited Shane's Castle in 1638. Though Rose was a staunch Presbyterian and Randal a committed Roman Catholic, love conquered all. The chief of the Macdonnells was installed as lord of Shane's Castle!

So dearly did Rose love Randal that she bestowed immortality upon him by renaming the town beside her castle - Randalstown. In 1683, Charles II approved her choice with a royal charter: "The town of...Main-Water...should be called for ever by the name of the Borough of Randalstown, and by that name...constituted a free borough".

One night in early nineteenth century Randalstown, Adam M'Clean was called to the deathbed of his old schoolmaster, Henry Mulhollan. It was the old man's dying wish that Adam should dig in his garden for an antique oak box. To Adam's astonishment, the box he unearthed housed the priceless 'Bell of the Will (of Saint Patrick)'.

The ancient Annals of Ulster record that 'relics of Patrick were placed in a shrine by Columcille, sixty years after his death. Three precious reliquaries were found in his tomb, to wit the Cup, the Gospel of the Angel, and the Bell of the Will'. Mulhollan's ancestors had been the hereditary keepers of Saint Patrick's Bell. Both shrine and bell are now in the possession of the Royal Irish Academy.

Randalstown

Randalstown is graced with two beautiful arched stone bridges spanning the River Maine. The low nine-arched road bridge is said to date from the eighteenth century. Railway mania in 1855 brought Randalstown its second spectacular architectural feature - the majestic eight-arched viaduct, seventy feet high above the river.

The celebrated architect Charles Lanyon designed the viaduct. However, he was of the opinion that it should be sited "a little higher up the river so as to place it in a direct line with the [railtrack] approaches on either side and thus avoid the awkward and dangerous turn at the western end". The builder, William Dargan, obviously didn't agree with Lanyon.

Though the railway closed in 1959, pedestrians and cyclists today enjoy specially constructed paths that cross the viaduct and afford interesting views of the town, river and adjacent parkland.

Beside the bridges is the site of the prehistoric and extensive iron works that gave the borough its original name of Iron Works (later changed to Main Water and subsequently Randalstown). From the mid-nineteenth century, the Old Bleach Linen Company occupied the site. Hand-painted woven table damasks originated here. Its high quality of household linens earned a global reputation as 'Old Bleach Linens'.

Mills for manufacturing paper were established at Ballygrooby in 1743 by Francis Joy, just a half dozen years after he had founded the oldest British daily newspaper, 'The Belfast News-Letter'.

During the Siege of Derry, Lord Antrim used the town as his military headquarters. In June 1798, the United Irishmen attacked and burned the Market House before advancing upon Antrim.

Beneath the bridges flows the River Maine - a favourite with anglers for its salmon, pike and dollaghan - which flows into Lough Neagh beside Shane's Castle estate. Across the river from the castle estate, both the mixed conifer Randalstown Forest and the adjacent Farrs Bay area are designated national nature reserves.

Randalstown Viaduct

The waters of Lough Neagh lap gently on the shores of 'the wood of wild garlic', anciently called Creamh-coille but known today as Cranfield. From the little harbour, local fishermen stalk eels and pollan. This is a place shrouded in mystery and tradition.

Near Churchtown Point, overlooking the bay, stand the romantic ruins of the tiny Church of Creamh-coille. The earliest record of the church dates back to 1306 though it was probably under the charge of Templepatrick's priory of the Knights of St. John from the late twelfth century. It has stood abandoned for almost four hundred years.

Cranfield's medieval church was built (perhaps intentionally) beside a well held sacred from ancient times by pagan tribes. Paganism remained a force to be reckoned with well into the Middle Ages. As Christianity adapted to the demands of pagan culture and society in order to become the dominant religion, the well was reputedly consecrated by St. Olcan. (St. Patrick is credited with having personally rescued the infant Olcan from death.) Down the years, each St. John's Eve (June 23rd), pilgrims would walk barefoot, thirteen times, around both church and well prior to bathing in the well.

St. Olcan's blessing of the well is commonly believed to have imparted to it fabled healing properties. Generations claimed that aches and pains were alleviated as votive rags (dipped in the well and tied to its overhanging bush) decayed. St. Olcan is said to rest in Cranfield's churchyard, in earth brought specially from Rome.

In times gone by, St. Olcan's Well was reported to overflow each May 1st, allowing small amber stones to appear mysteriously in the water. Lough fishermen and emigrants insisted that wearing these stones provided protection against drowning. These talismans were sought eagerly also to protect women during childbirth and homes against fire or burglary. The stones are crystals of gypsum, not unique to Cranfield.

Cranfield

Tannoy speakers dotted around Toome once filled the air with strains of Sinatra, Crosby, The Ink Spots and The Andrews Sisters. US comedian and film star, Bob Hope, arrived to entertain the United States 8th Air Force stationed in the area during the Second World War.

Heavy bombers - the B-17 Flying Fortress and B-24 Liberator - rehearsed here for bombing missions in Europe. The sky was crowded with Mustangs, Thunderbolts, Hurricanes and Spitfires engaged in mock dog-fights.

The story is still told locally of how a military jeep, careering along a small country road, smacked straight into a donkey and cart, catapulting the old man aboard the cart many yards down the road. The Yankee driver who leapt out of the jeep was appalled to find the donkey in great distress, its legs badly mangled. Without hesitation, he withdrew his revolver and at once blasted the beast out of its misery.

Having witnessed the execution, the old man endeavoured to struggle away from the scene. Suddenly noticing the old fellow, the serviceman raced over, smoke still curling from the barrel of his gun.

"Heck! A'm real sorry, old man, about your mule. A guess you're not feeling too good either?"

Keeping a wary eye on the still-drawn six-shooter, the old man summoned sufficient strength to answer that he had never felt better in all his life!

Toome's wartime episode lasted only two or three years. Since time immemorial, however, thousands of miles from Toome in the dark depths of the salty Sargasso Sea, tiny elvers have been caught by the Gulf Stream and wafted across the North Atlantic into the River Bann. Upstream, in the great freshwater sea of Lough Neagh, they develop into brown eels. A dozen years later comes the time for fully mature silver eels to return to their distant spawning ground.

At Toome, however, nylon nets across the Lower Bann scoop a percentage of the migrating silver eels, which are promptly boxed and exported live the same day to continental restaurants. The annual catch - Europe's greatest source of eels - is worth several million pounds.

Toome

The skyline north-east of Antrim is cloaked in the emerald shades of mixed conifer forests. Prevailing south-westerly winds racing in from the Atlantic and across Lough Neagh climb some three hundred feet over Tardree mountain, guaranteeing the spot freedom from drought.

The Forestry Division of the Department of Agriculture first covered the high moorland of Tardree and Carnearny mountains with conifer trees in 1929: Norway and Sitka (North American) Spruce, Japanese Larch, Lodge Pole Pine, Noble and Grand Silver Firs. (Hardwood trees would have grown much more slowly.) Their roots held the soil firm, absorbing the heavy rainfall here and releasing it only slowly into streams flowing down to the lough. It took about sixty years before the first planting was mature for harvesting.

Visitors enjoy free access to Tardree's attractive, tranquil forest walks and picnic areas. Panoramic views embrace the Mourne and Sperrin mountain ranges, Lough Neagh and central Ulster, Slemish and the blue hills of Antrim.

At the Ladyhill approach to the forest at Carnearny, a forest path winds round an old quarry and skirts the front of a rocky outcrop. In the middle of the rockface is a feature known as 'The Devil's Wishing Chair'. Tradition holds that here, in ancient times, pagan clansmen assembled to swear allegiance to their chieftain, seated upon his inaugural stone chair. (Majestic views were also afforded from a somewhat similar structure, locally called 'The Priest's Chair', on Donegore Hill.)

A geological nature reserve has been created within Tardree's rhyolite quarry. 'Tardree Stone' is a highly distinctive and attractive igneous rock, peculiar to this summit. This very ancient stone escaped being engulfed by the successive lava flows that created the much younger and familiar black basalt of the Antrim Plateau. Many of Antrim's important buildings erected in the nineteenth century were built with the black basalt but decorously and expensively enhanced with dressings of distinctive Tardree Stone.

Tardree Forest

There is no freshwater lake in the British Isles as extensive as the hundred and fifty three square miles of Lough Neagh. The lough's catchment area covers forty three per cent of Northern Ireland.

Daily abstraction of millions of gallons of water from the lough for Antrim and Belfast, for drinking purposes, causes less than a one inch drop in level over a year.

Oceanography observations on the lough near Crumlin, conducted by University College London in the mid-twentieth century, laid important foundations for international studies of wave-produced energy. However, geologists' arguments that Lough Neagh originated as a glacial puddle when the last Ice Age melted away, cut little ice with those who advocate a more magical origin.

The classic tale recounts how, when the legendary Finn McCool was resting after constructing his celebrated Causeway, in a fit of pique he hurled an Antrim sod at a rival giant in England. Unfortunately, Finn miscalculated both the velocity and trajectory of his missile. The sod fell half way across the Irish Sea (to form the Isle of Man), the resulting splash filling the hole left here to form Lough Neagh!

A colourful Gaelic legend tells how Ecca, a southern prince, arrived here with his followers and commenced constructing his palace and city, complete with monastic buildings and round towers. He assigned a woman of the tribe to tend a troublesome well, over which Ecca had secured a flap. When the woman became negligent and forgot to secure the flap properly, water overflowed the well, drowning Ecca and all his tribe and their dwellings and finally submerging the wide central plain of Ulster. Ecca lives on, apparently, as 'Lord of the Underworld' and the great Lough of Ecca (or 'Lough n'Ecca') has eventually become known as Lough Neagh.

On Lough Neagh's banks where the fisherman strays,
When the clear, cold eve's declining,
He sees the round towers of other days
In the waves beneath him shining.

'Let Erin Remember', Thomas Moore

Lough Neagh

The People of Antrim

The earliest known human settlers in Ireland set up camp along the Lower River Bann and at Toome Bay. Man first ventured up the river in dugout tree trunks about nine thousand years ago, from the north and west of Britain. Along the northern shore of the greatest freshwater lake in these islands, Lough Neagh, these fisherfolk dropped anchor. Salmon and eel a-plenty were on the menu.

Mesolithic Age settlers, with no agriculture or husbandry, appear to have been wholly preoccupied simply striving to survive. For some three thousand years they enjoyed the freedom of our district. Then new neighbours arrived from the Middle East. Fortunately the climate of Mid-Antrim then was warmer and drier.

These early farmers migrated inland to the uplands. Giant elk and wolf-packs roamed the inhospitable valleys where dense primeval forest grew on the comparatively heavier soils. On such conspicuous summits as Lyles Hill and Donegore (Templepatrick), these Neolithic (New Stone Age: 4000-2000 B.C.)

people put down their roots. They sowed wheat to make bread and kept early breeds of cattle, sheep, pigs, cats and dogs. Their weaving of cloth and spinning of flax into linen ushered in a textile tradition which would characterise the area right down to modern times.

The technology of finely-polished stone provided Neolithic man with the means to fell tracts of the extensive forests for farming; his arrow and axe heads and flint implements are still often found locally.

The finest and most extensive Neolithic settlement sites in these islands have been uncovered near Templepatrick. Fortifications and artifacts in abundance found on Donegore Hill offer unique evidence of the way of life in Ireland five or six thousand years ago. Great wooden and fortified roundhouses have been excavated at both Donegore and Rathbeg. Within sight of Donegore, evidence has been found of spacious Neolithic occupation of the smooth, oval dome of Lyles Hill.

Being sufficiently advanced as farmers, these people had time for activity other than merely ensuring their own survival. Enormous quantities of decorated pottery, discovered at this grassy thirteen acre hilltop fort, testify to an important manufacturing industry developed by these Neolithic businessmen.

Other intriguing sites of ceremonial or religious significance have been discovered, including Langford Lodge (Crumlin), Dunadry and Parkgate. Local archaeological excavations have regularly unearthed an enormous variety of Neolithic community constructions, megalithic passage-graves, cairns, standing stones and stone circles.

Behind Donegore towers the mass of Browndod. Ancient trackways and haunting prehistoric stone monuments crown this lonely summit. An aged 'fairy thorn' tree guards a spectacular, dramatically long and horned, collective burial chamber tomb. The Victorians rather misleadingly dubbed this a 'Druid's Altar'. From a wedge-shaped forecourt, the forty feet long Altar reveals four burial chambers of Western Neolithic peoples. Such organised burials provide the earliest evidence of the dead being revered.

The finest Bronze Age standing stone of its kind in the British Isles commands a magnificent panorama of the countryside north-east of Parkgate village. The enigmatic, five feet tall Holestone megalith is pierced with a quite mysterious, countersunk hole. Perhaps its use in recent centuries as a 'Stone of Love' by troth-plighting couples echoes some ancient rite for solemnising marriages or treaties by the joining of hands through the hole?

Nine chambered megaliths, rising in height successively over a distance of forty-five feet, form the impressive passage-grave of Carn Grainne at Templepatrick. Legend has it that Princess Grainne slept here during her flight from Celtic warriors who pursued her across Ireland. Apparently, Grainne ran away from home (the royal palace of Tara) when her regal father arranged for her to marry the aged Ulster giant, Finn McCool.

Following in Grainne's footsteps, Celtic-speaking Gaels moved north into the Antrim area from about 600 B.C. (We call them Celts, after the Greek term 'Keltoi', signifying a people 'different from us'.) One of their tribal thrones - the 'Devil's Wishing Chair' - is cut into the basaltic face of Carnearny Mountain above Antrim. There, where pagan clansmen assembled to subject themselves to their chieftain, you may scan mountain ranges from Mourne to Donegal, to where land and sky join and you can see neither the birth of one nor the death of the other.

The first 'road' in Ireland - winding from the ancient Celtic capital of Tara in the south to Ireland's oldest fort - Dunseverick - on the north Antrim coast, tripped through the valley of the Sixmilewater river. Highway number two, running west from Carrickfergus to the ford at Toome, intersected where the original Antrim settlement would be established.

The area's climatic conditions and rich lowland soil proved ideal for supporting various cereals and, in particular, corn production. As well as being rather partial to the brewing of beer, Celts needed good fodder to rear horses of stamina and quality. In naming this ancient kingdom 'Dal nAraida' (Dalriada), the Celtic 'Araide' may be connected with the Latin 'Epo-redial', meaning horse-breakers. Pursuing a pastoral existence as 'cowlords' and horse-breeders was something that Celts inherited from the prehistoric ages. Horse-drawn chariots served as both principal modes of transport and deadly war machines.

Ireland's greatest concentration of Celtic earthworks is crowded into the Antrim area. These early-Christian farmsteads (raths) were ringed with earthen and stone ramparts. A wooden fence on top of the encircling rampart kept livestock within the enclosure. The surrounding ditch served to keep out hungry wolves and greedy neighbours. The number of cattle a man (or woman) owned, determined wealth and social status.

Two of the very few raths in state care are the thousand year old Spring Farm Rath in Antrim town and the complex site at Ballywee, high on the hill above Parkgate village. At Ballywee, survive the excavated remains of a rectangular stone farmhouse amid a variety of ring forts, enclosures and a veritable honeycomb of underground souterrain 'caves'.

The souterrain was one of the keys to the Celts' survival: a sophisticated underground chamber that served both as a refuge from attackers and as a highly efficient deep-freeze. With huge lintel stones capping dry-stone walled passageways, these earth covered constructions were insulated and well disguised. Ireland's only known two-chamber and two-storey souterrain was discovered at Bog Head, just outside Antrim town. Such was their expert construction, souterrains have survived intact for a millennium. Some, however, have succumbed to the weight of modern farm machinery, much to the consternation of the farmers involved in such disasters.

Two cyclopean structures, each with double ramparts and twin trenches, endure at Rathenraw (Antrim) and at Ballywoodock (between the hills of Browndod and Donegore). Perhaps their owners were unusually wealthy Celts or opted for twin defences to counter the threat of new, long-range slingshot weaponry.

Rathmore (close to the Rathbeg M2 roundabout) is an oval ringfort, 161 feet across and 16 feet high, with an underground passageway leading down an incredible 428 feet to a well in a large cave. Its name translates as the 'Great Fort', not because of its physical size (for there is little to distinguish it from the 30,000 other raths in Ireland) but because here was once the royal seat of the 'Great One'- the king of Dalriada.

High-king Diarmait mac Cerball (548-64 A.D.) was the last of the great pagan monarchs of Ireland to reside in the ancient palace at Tara. At the time when Ireland was moving from a pagan Iron Age society towards Christianity, Diarmait persisted in celebrating pagan feasts. When Saint Ruadan of Lorrha responded by cursing Tara, King Diarmait took the hint, abandoned Tara and moved into Rathmore. He succeeded to the Dalriadan 'throne' in 565 A.D. and later further distinguished himself by laying the foundation stone of Clonmacnoise monastery, one of the great Irish centres of holiness and learning.

Rathmore was the scene of mayhem and murder in 687 A.D. Hostile invaders led by a Northumbrian lord slew the Dalriadan chief "and a great number of the Irish along with him at the battlefield of Rathmore". A great assembly of warrior chiefs gathered at Rathmore in 987 A.D., among them a future high-king of Ireland. The place continued as a royal seat until 1004 when, according to the ancient annals, Brian Boru "marched from Armagh to Rath-more, in Moy-line, until he carried away the hostages of Dalaradia with him".

As well as the prefix 'rath', many local placenames preserve the Celtic 'dun' to signify a fort: Dunadry was, perhaps, the 'middle fort' between the celebrated regal hill of Tara in the south and the ancient north coast promontory fortress of Dunseverick.

Saint Patrick is reputed to have made a personal appearance in the district in the early fifth century. Wheeling into town aboard a two-horse-powered Celtic shamrock chariot, Patrick was intent on advising local warrior pagans to love their neighbours. Though Glenavy men scoffed and chased Patrick away, men of Antrim were eventually inspired to establish a grand rush-thatched, oaken monastic house, around 495 A.D. It survived the great plague of the 660s and attacks from hostile Gaelic tribes.

The monastic site was named 'Aentrobh', signifying 'the one ridge': the site lay on the western base of a distinctive hilly ridge which wriggled its way from Tardree mountain down to Ram's Island at Lough Neagh's Sandy Bay.

Some six hundred monks established Aentrobh

monastery as the area's first distinctive centre for civilisation. Here would have been a refectory and monks' cells made of sticks plastered with mud and thatched. Probably too there was a library and scriptorium, as well as farm buildings to store fodder and house animals. Typically, monks would study Latin, Greek, Astronomy, Mathematics, Music and the Scriptures. The skins of calves (vellum) would have provided writing materials on which scribes could copy the Gospels and Psalms, using quill pens made from goose feathers.

Though eventually consumed by fire and abandoned by 1147 A.D., two intriguing traces remain today of this great monastic site. Then as now, the most prominent landmark of the district is the uniquely Irish, free-standing round tower, one of the finest surviving. Its high doorway suggests that one function may have been to provide a place of refuge. Though its original purpose remains unknown, it could have served both practical and symbolic functions. At the tower's base stands what probably once acted as the monastery's kitchen preparation table - a gigantic 'bullaun' stone.

A few miles distant at Muckamore, an important and prosperous monastic seminary (without any round tower) was founded on 'the great field of adoration' (as St. Patrick would have known it) in 550 A.D. Some two or three hundred Augustinian students studied here. The British Museum preserves extracts from the register of one of Muckamore Abbey's priors. Muckamore Abbey (unlike Aentrobh monastery) was plundered and damaged by Viking raiders, who terrorised Northern Europe from the eighth to the tenth centuries.

The short swords of the native Irish were no match for Viking battle-axes but, nonetheless, the Norsemen could not destroy the rule of the Irish kings. Brian Boru, shortly after visiting Rathmore, smashed the Viking invasion of Ireland with his victory at the Battle of Clontarf. That ushered in a new era of peace when monasteries could be rebuilt and regain their prestige, power and wealth.

But it was the Vikings who didn't come here who, in the longer term, exerted a more profound effect on the greater Antrim area. Danish Vikings had colonised northern France in the tenth century. These 'North Men' became known as Normans (of Normandy). In 1066 they invaded and conquered England. By the twelfth century, as Anglo-Normans, they turned their attention towards Ireland.

A venturous, young freebooter, John de Courcy (the Anglo-Norman conqueror of East Ulster) began building Carrickfergus Castle in the 1180s. The rich pastoral and arable valley of the Amhuin na Fiodh ('River of the Woods') - now called the Sixmilewater river - was quickly subdued and settled by these warrior knights.

Within weeks of their arrival, they consolidated their hold of the land by erecting hundreds of distinctive steep-sided plum-pudding-like earthen mounds (or mottes); each ringed with a trench and crowned with a wooden archery tower. The adjacent open space, also protected by a ditch and fence, formed a 'bailey' for housing people, animals and produce. Ancient raths usually offered attractive sites for Norman redevelopment, as at Rathenraw (Antrim), Rathmore and Donegore. A motte at Toome, a traditional fording point of Ulster's longest river, the Bann, guarded the greater Antrim area from western attack.

The Sixmilewater offered a clean and dependable water supply, so where it could be forded easily, a short distance above its confluence with Lough Neagh, de Courcy constructed his motte-castle of 'Antrum'. ('Antrum', like the monastic 'Aentrobh' before it, signified 'a ridge' which wound from Tardree Mountain to Lough Neagh's Sandy Bay.) This motte was initially constructed as a huge sandcastle (using Lough Neagh sand) and subsequently covered with earth.

Rural Antrim, eminently suitable for the intense agricultural productivity of Anglo-Norman settlers, was organised and settled by 1226. Their feudal pattern of mixed farming took firm hold across the countryside. Land was improved and farmed by the religious orders that the Normans encouraged and supported. At Rathmore they founded a small priory and the abbey at Muckamore they rebuilt and rededicated to Ss. Mary and Colman.

The Account Rolls of Elizabeth de Burgh (1353-60) offer a glimpse of this early medieval 'Antrum villae': a castle, court, tower, orchards, brewers, corn mills, and "a cow sold for 4s. 6d". The territory they called their 'bailiwick of Antrum' emerges as county Antrim in the 1333 inquisition. The pre-eminent family of the bailiwick, ruling from the Manor of Donegore, was the Savages (who later provided seneschals for Ulster).

The Irish had insufficient strength to resist the Anglo-Norman occupation. Some three thousand Irish were slain near Donegore when their primitive slings and axes proved ineffectual against archers and mail-clad, iron-helmeted knights wielding lances and swords. After that, the O'Neill clan waited, in an aloof antagonism, west of the Bann.

Protecting Antrim, two Norman galleys patrolled Lough Neagh by order of King John. But the days of Norman rule were to be ended unexpectedly, not by the Irish but by Scots.

When the various kings of Ireland could not agree about which one of themselves to elect to the high-kingship, the king of Ulster suggested that Edward Bruce (whose brother, Robert, had successfully defended Scotland from the English) should be appointed to drive the Norman menace from Ireland.

In 1315, Edward Bruce's Bannockburn veterans overran the Norman mottes at Rathmore and Donegore in a major and bloody battle fought around Rathbeg (where the motorway runs today). With the expulsion of the Norman barons, and the thistle warriors' invasion ending later in disarray, the Clannaboy branch of the Irish O'Neills seized the opportunity to retake Mid-Antrim. To commemorate an O'Neill queen who drowned in the Sixmilewater river, the Barony of Antrum was renamed 'Masaregna'. The name survives today as Massereene.

Beside the river, opposite the old Norman motte, the O'Neills founded a Franciscan Friary of the Brothers of Masarine, endowing it with thirty acres of gently rolling countryside stretching south along the lough shore. Muckamore Abbey obtained a grant from Henry VII to hold an annual horse fair at Oldstone each 12th July; this became the largest and most important horse fair throughout Ulster. Henry VIII, however, robbed Muckamore of its abbey, lands and churches with his dissolution of monasteries.

The days of saints and scholars were at an end. Elizabethan English adventurers had developed a hungry eye for the rich farmland of Mid-Antrim. First, however, the O'Neills would have to be conquered.

The campaign to establish English control necessitated fortifying Massereene at Antrim, principally as a naval base for operations across Lough Neagh. The English were prepared for tough frontier warfare, such as they were also directing against North American Indians. In the Earl of Essex expedition, sent by Elizabeth I in 1573, was a young captain, Hugh Clotworthy. Unknown to Clotworthy, he was destined to found an important dynastic family which would endure about Antrim down to the twentieth century.

Landing at Carrickfergus, Clotworthy's orders were to march his troops six miles inland. There they would encounter a river - or 'water' - which would lead them down to the great inland sea of Lough Neagh. Hence, the eighteen-mile long 'River of the Woods' became commonly known as the 'Six-mile Water'. The lough was to become the operational nerve-centre for English troops shipping ammunition and supplies from Carrickfergus to Tyrone.

Within a few miles of where Shane MacBrian O'Neill built his Shane's Castle in 1580, and near where the Sixmilewater enters the lough, the English pitched camp, exactly where the Normans before them had erected their Antrum castle in the Middle Ages. A number of timber houses were built to store military equipment and provisions. For its fortifications and strategic location, the fortress that Clotworthy constructed became a vital English stronghold. Sections of its sturdy perimeter defenses still exist.

A new Antrim town began to take shape between the Elizabethans' military fort and their Anglican parish church. By 1596, a typically English high street, with timbered buildings, was beginning to appear. O'Neills dubbed the place 'Gall-Antrum', (the Antrim of the English foreigner).

Once his military HQ at Antrim was secured, Clotworthy constructed a Lough Neagh navy to attack Irish settlements at Randalstown and Toome (as well as for supplying troops stationed at Mountjoy in Tyrone and Charlemont on the Blackwater). O'Neills responded by navigating the lough in light barques and curragh boats to launch hit-and-run reprisals.

The old Gaelic order eventually collapsed when the Irish chieftains either submitted or fled abroad in 1603. Essex Man ruled Mid-Antrim. Sir Hugh Clotworthy was knighted, appointed county high sheriff and awarded control of Massereene lands. For first lady of the little stone keep he was erecting as his 'Castle of Antrim', Clotworthy chose Lady Marian Langford. Her father (Sir Roger) acquired Muckamore's old abbey and its four hundred acre demesne. Fellow captain, Sir Robert Norton, acquired the site of the medieval priory at Templepatrick to erect his Castle Norton. Shortly afterwards, Norton sold the property to Captain Henry Upton, giving the edifice its present name of Castle Upton.

The promise of peace and prosperity for Mid-Antrim attracted 'adventurous spirits, from Scotland, whose finances had run low, glad of the opportunity of a chance in a new country; new, yet within sight of the old'. Given also the religious persecution of these (Southern Upland) Scots by King James I, the liberty of conscience enjoyed in Ulster was a significant stimulus for immigration. The Clotworthies were enterprising landlords and privately encouraged the influx of English and Scots settlers.

Lowland Scots erected clusters of thatched cabins across the countryside. A new 'Scotch Quarter' (Church Street) attached itself to Antrim town, expanding the population to some three or four hundred. Their small homes echoed to the sounds of spinning wheels and the clatter of weavers' shuttles. Several also pursued livings as glovers, bakers, pewterers, tanners, nailers and millers. One miller's son, William King, born in Antrim in 1650, later became

Archbishop of Dublin. Jacobites once imprisoned him for treason after disclosing information to the Duke Of Schomberg during the Williamite wars. "The archbishop couldn't help being born in Antrim, but in his autobiography he could avoid mentioning the fact- and did so!" noted one local writer.

As well as transporting into Antrim their traditional socio-economic way of life, the Scots settlers carried with them the enduring legacy of the doctrine of Presbyterianism. The puritanical Clotworthy family encouraged the settlement of preachers of Scottish Presbyterian (and English Puritan) conviction. A plaque inscribed 'Ecclesia Scotica' still adorns their meeting house in Crumlin. The Antrim Presbyterian congregation, formed by 1619, remains one of the oldest in Ireland.

The Great Revival of 1625 established the Sixmilewater valley as 'the cradle of Irish Presbyterianism'. Rev. Josias Welsh - the grandson of the great Scottish Reformer, John Knox - was installed as personal chaplain at Castle Upton, Templepatrick. Welsh's imposing tomb is clearly marked in the old burial ground beside Castle Upton.

Presbyterian ways then differed somewhat from practice today. Church seats had to be rented and all accounts and arrears paid at an entrance gate before admission to the church would be granted. After the forgeries were separated out, the 'offerings' taken up at every service supported the poor of the district. Communion services were celebrated with gallons of wine and rum, the preacher being treated to a particularly tasty but secret brew called 'rum and scrub'!

The Scots also imported a distinctive accent and vernacular that would endure and characterise the sinew of Mid-Antrim speech to the present day. In the 'Cottier's Death and Burial', weaver folk-poet James Orr (1770-1816) describes how, when the preacher arrives, the "Scotch-tongued rustics" attempt "to quate braid Scotch, a task that foils their art".

Local businessman, William Edmundson held in Antrim the first meeting of what became the Society of Friends in Ireland, in 1636. Said Methodist founder, John Wesley, during one of three visits to Antrim: "His opinions I leave; but what a spirit was there! Could mistakes send such a man as this to Hell? Not so. I am so far from believing this that I scruple not to say- Let my soul be with the soul of William Edmundson!" Since 1685, an old walled graveyard, exclusively for Quakers, has mouldered silently off the main road between Antrim and Muckamore.

A letter to a resident of Antrim in 1641 sparked off one of the bloodiest events in Irish history. A plot by the Irish to launch a surprise attack on Dublin Castle was disclosed by a conspirator in a letter to Owen O'Connolly, a friend at Antrim Castle. However, the writer had misjudged his man. O'Connolly's timely warning saved the castle and made him a national hero, though it did not prevent rebellion breaking out elsewhere.

During the 1641 Rebellion, as the Irish torched country cottages and fields of corn, local Protestant tenants sought the protection of military garrisons at Antrim, Templepatrick and Shane's Castle. Horrific massacres (by both sides) were recorded, particularly in Ulster. The castle at Antrim managed to survive repeated assaults over several months. In one attack, Turlough O'Neill led four thousand Irish against Antrim in February 1642. Troops garrisoned in Antrim pursued retreating rebels, killing about eighty of the Irish tenants of the Castle Upton estate. Where rebels sought sanctuary - whether in the small stone church attached to Antrim round tower or the ancient Dundesart monastery, near the Crumlin river - the English nonetheless shelled mercilessly. The village of Kilbride was completely destroyed.

Parliament enlarged the Antrim garrison and expanded the Lough Neagh fleet by a dozen large armed gunboats. A major Anglo-Irish naval battle on the lough in 1643 secured victory for those garrisoned at Antrim. Peace was short lived, however. Catastrophe threatened from two quite unexpected quarters.

Sir John Clotworthy could scarcely have imagined the consequences when he introduced the young Oliver Cromwell to the English parliament. Their friendship was one casualty when the Long Parliament split in two. As a Conservative loyal to King Charles 1, Sir John found himself opposed by Cromwell's radical Independents. After England's civil war, when Clotworthy protested at the arrest and execution of Charles 1, Cromwell had Sir John charged with high treason and imprisoned. As Clotworthy was a royalist opposed to Cromwell's Commonwealth republic, Cromwellian soldiers had no hesitation in sequestrating Antrim Castle.

The following year, 1649, a Scottish and royalist Covenanting army marched on Antrim. After defeating Cromwellian troops in battle at Dunadry, the Scots avengers attacked Cromwellian-held Antrim. In the words of one of their officers, they "summoned the town to yield to the King. But those within the Castle, one of Cromwell's captains with his company...returned answer that they would not yield the Castle; on which the town was assaulted and burned". It took over seventy years to rebuild Antrim.

The Restoration of the English monarchy allowed for

the restoration of Sir John Clotworthy to his Antrim estate and for his elevation to the title of First Viscount of Massereene. He was also made Baron of Lough Neagh, with ownership of the lough, its islands and fishing rights. His 'old frowning keep' at Antrim was transformed into a stately mansion, set amid fashionable Anglo-Dutch water gardens. A thousand acres along the eastern shore of Lough Neagh were added as a deer park. Whereas most of the Massereene dynasty was to be buried in the crypt of Antrim Parish Church, Sir John Clotworthy was accorded Saint Patrick's Cathedral in Dublin as his final resting place.

Massereene's estates - some 45,000 acres - stretched from Dunluce in the north to Tipperary in the south of Ireland. His local estate fell into the hands of King James II's Jacobite army on its march from Belfast to Coleraine. The coronation of William III of Orange, however, enabled the Massereenes once again to regain the Antrim estate.

Phoenix-like, a new town of Antrim rose from its old ashes during the early years of the eighteenth century. Reconstruction work was completed, in 1726, with the remodelling of the old rough masonry Market House into one of the richest classical buildings of Florentine style in Ireland. The town's Market Square became a focal point for fairs and livestock markets.

Six bad harvests at the start of the eighteenth century encouraged the exodus of many Antrim small farmers to the North American colonies. Since the 1630s, the local rural economy had hinged on an interdependence of subsistence farming and linen weaving. The celebrated travel writer, Arthur Young, who visited Antrim in 1776, found that "the linen manufacture spreads over the whole country, consequently the farms are very small, being nothing but patches for the convenience of weavers".

Subsequent recessions in the local linen industry, rocketing prices and rents and more bad harvests prompted evictions and more departures for the New World, where many of the Ulster-Scots became celebrated frontiersmen and significant historical figures. Eight US Presidents could trace their descent back to county Antrim. Antrim emigrants founded some nine 'New Antrims' in North America.

The American War of Independence prevented any further emigration for much of the rest of the century. If the people of Mid-Antrim harboured any grievances - and Presbyterians and all other Dissenters (Quakers, Baptists and, later, Methodists) as well as Roman Catholics had plenty - they would have to be resolved at home.

The Episcopal Church of Ireland, as the established

body, created a deep social unrest. By the archaic Test Act (1704), the only citizens who could hold public office were those who took the communion sacrament according to rites of the established church. Punitive restrictions by the English government also cramped the industrial and commercial interests and potential of Presbyterian Ulster, (thereby promoting economic growth in Britain). The vast majority of small farmers about Antrim were Presbyterians who were not only charged heavy rents by their Church of Ireland landlords but were obliged to financially support the Anglican church in addition to their own. The disaffected were bent on breaking the traditional political power of the governing Anglican class by challenging the aristocratic Massereenes at the ballot box.

Paradoxically, it was one of the Massereene lords who practically destroyed the family's local power. The 2nd Earl - something of an eccentric rogue - drifted about Europe, squandering the family fortune and was imprisoned in France for eighteen years. He would have served much longer had not the Parisian mob liberated him during the French Revolution.

After the Earl's second marriage, to a former mistress, the couple were visiting Dublin when their pet dog died. Following a special wake for the pet, a grand funeral procession (with the dog's remains in a handsome lead coffin) wound its way northwards to Antrim. All local dog owners were commanded to attend the funeral service at Antrim Castle, with their dogs sporting mourning scarves!

Even if the Earl's antics had not been bringing into greater and greater disrepute the name of Massereene, the political allegiance of local farmers, tenants and clergy was more and more attracted to the entrepreneuring Thompson family of Greenmount.

The Thompsons were Scots Presbyterian businessmen with extensive estates not just around Antrim but as far distant as the West Indies. They contested several parliamentary elections as Independents. Though they gave the Massereenes some close contests and lodged protests of 'unfair influence and bribery' by the aristocratic landlords, the Thompsons remained unsuccessful. Here, as elsewhere, the constitutional movement for radical reform failed. Notwithstanding, the oppressive civic and religious laws of the unrepresentative Anglo-Irish parliament eventually provoked a bloody insurrection.

That the violent and determined 1798 Rebellion of United Irishmen was fought in Antrim (against government forces) almost exclusively by Presbyterians, distinguishes this conflict from other '98 uprisings in the south of Ireland. Political, religious and economic persecution had already driven hundreds of thousands of Scots-Irish (Ulster Presbyterians) to the New World. There, in 1783, they had helped to win the war against England for their own democratic independence; the lesson was not lost on their unenfranchised kinfolk back at home in Ulster.

Presbyterians had admiration also for the French Revolution (1789); abolition of tithes, establishment of religious equality and a national assembly representative of the people. Radicals now demanded absolute political and religious equality and freedom for citizens of every religion and class in Ireland. They saw nothing but good in the simple desire to obtain their democratic 'rights of man': improvement of living standards and conferring on every man an equal right to vote. To promote such a campaign, many local branches were formed of the country-wide Society of United Irishmen.

The United Irishmen, initially, sought peaceful, political reform of the unrepresentative Anglo-Irish parliament in Dublin. However, events soon forced the organisation into an underground revolutionary movement. The government remained unsympathetic to calls for reform of parliament and harassed suspected radicals. It undermined Catholic support for the United Irish cause through the enactment of Catholic relief acts. This, together with the overwhelming numbers of Presbyterians in Mid-Antrim, meant that those who would ultimately rebel at Antrim would be almost exclusively Presbyterian.

Tremendous tension built following the government execution of a prominent Antrim Presbyterian farmer, William Orr. Arrested after publishing a call for absolute political and religious equality and freedom for all citizens, Orr's execution (October 1797) created a martyr and rallied supporters to the war-cry "Remember Orr!" During the early summer of 1798, rebellion exploded at Antrim.

County Governor, Lord O'Neill of Shane's Castle, had summoned a meeting of the county's magistrates at Antrim Market House on June 7th, 1798. Henry Joy McCracken, (who had family connections with Killead and Randalstown), chose the same date for a surprise United Irish assault on Antrim to capture the magistrates and use them as hostages for the release of imprisoned rebel sympathisers.

McCracken hoped for military, naval and financial support from the National Assembly of France (which had been at war with England since 1793). To attack Antrim, he reckoned also on the support of some 22,000 of Ulster's United Irishmen. Though Antrim had a garrison of just 100 soldiers, the element of surprise turned out not to be McCracken's.

In the event, French support did not materialise and McCracken's call to arms realised a force of only 3,500 rebel Irishmen; the expected remainder 'reported sick' on the day! Unknown to McCracken, the military had learned of his proposed attack and the stage had been prepared for a brutal engagement.

Early on the morning of June 7th, 1798, rebels unearthed two brass, six-pounder cannon hidden in the Old Presbyterian Meeting House at Templepatrick. Reinforced by United Irish from Crumlin, Doagh, Parkgate, Killead, Muckamore and East Antrim districts, the rebels marched upon Antrim.

The Battle of Antrim was fought along the length of the town's main street. The main party of rebels advanced through the strongly Presbyterian Scotch Quarter (Church Street). Simultaneously, from the other side of town, some 1500 comrades from Toome and Randalstown were expected to enter via Castle Street. What transpired, in reality, was a different matter.

When an advance party of military reinforcements arrived from Lisburn, the United Irish in the Scotch Quarter sought cover behind the wall of the strategically sited parish churchyard. The cavalry's furious charge towards the Scotch Quarter was answered with some four hundred musket-balls and a six-pound round shot from one of the United Irishmen's cannon. Trapped in the confined roadway beside the churchyard, with superior numbers of rebel pike-men surrounding them, the military fought desperately to escape. Seventeen soldiers died, thirty were wounded and forty horses were slain. Amid the mayhem, the county governor, Lord O'Neill, was assassinated.

Surviving cavalry retreated along the main street to safety behind the Market House, at the entrance to Castle Street. Coincidentally, a reserve contingent of rebels also sought cover in Castle Street. The cavalry promptly extended their retreat, towards the Randalstown Road.

United Irishmen arriving just then, from an assault upon Randalstown, were not to know that the cavalry who came charging towards them from Castle Street were, in fact, in hasty retreat! Disunited Randalstown men, consequently, took to their heels across the fields.

Military reinforcements from Belfast and Lisburn appeared and their shelling liberated the town. In the aftermath of battle, soldiers sacked the town and pursued rebels throughout the district. Some hundreds of the dead and dying littered the streets of Antrim. The ground floor of the Market House served as a temporary morgue. Mass graves rapidly filled near the lough shore.

Randalstown and Templepatrick were looted and then torched by the military. A militia captain mused in his diary: "It fell to my lot to set fire to Randalstown, which was soon effectually done by sending artillerymen in different directions with portfires. The houses, being mostly thatch, were soon ablaze. Only those who witness such distressing scenes can form any idea of them. How far such measures are politic, Government ought best to know".

Two central arches of the old wooden bridge at Toome (constructed by Lord O'Neill just six years previous) were hastily dismantled by rebels to thwart further military pursuits.

A few weeks later, Henry Joy McCracken was executed at Belfast's Market House and upon its roof were displayed the severed heads of several of his Antrim comrades. Ironically, shortly afterwards and from that same place, the legislative union of Ireland and Great Britain was proclaimed; the old Irish parliament which the rebels had sought to reform was abolished. With the 1801 Act of Union, however, Britain effectively appointed itself the target for future grievances in Ireland!

What if the United Irishmen had won? If Napoleon had sent troops, might things have transpired as the United Irishmen had hoped? Might they not have made Ulster (or Ireland) merely a province of an expanding French Empire?

In '98 we armed again
To right some things that we thought wrang;
We got so little for our pains
It's no worth mindin' in a song
James Campbell (1758-1818)

Campbell was one of the Sixmilewater valley's well-read, self-educated rural bards. Their local reading societies and book clubs were considered so radical and seditious that they became a target of the yeomanry during and after the 1798 Uprising.

While working at their cottage looms, inkhorn and paper were always at the ready. These 'Rhyming Weavers', as they called themselves, composed spontaneous verses in their vernacular Scotch about spinning wheels, local places, the seasons, birds, teapots, potatoes, etc. Some of their published collections attracted as many (and sometimes many more) subscribers than works by their famous Scottish contemporary, Robert Burns.

A Lyles Hill schoolmaster with literary ambitions, Samuel Thompson (1766-1816), who personally visited Burns, dedicated his first volume of vernacular poems to 'Mr Robert Burns, the celebrated Ayrshire poet'. Parkgate's Sir Samuel Ferguson ('Ireland's greatest poet', as W.B. Yeats described him) reviewing the work of the Sixmilewater rustic bards, claimed: "Robert Burns' own parish was not more deeply imbued with the love of song than the central district of the county of Antrim".

The socio-economic conditions, which had long helped to preserve old traditions and cultural patterns in Antrim rural society, were weakened during the nineteenth century by the advent of National Schools, railways and emigration.

Antrim's 2,183 population at the start of the nineteenth century was served by shops of prospering tradespeople, which fronted the main street. Behind this respectable facade, however, discreetly tucked out of sight in countless little alleyways or entries, the labouring class rented pitifully small stone cabins.

Stepping off Antrim's main street and through Pogue's Entry, today's visitor is whisked back a hundred years and more. Here, perfectly preserved two-storey, nineteenth century white-washed brickwork houses - the homes once of a simple ragman and chimney sweep - gaze across the narrow cobbled alley at an early eighteenth century, single-storey labourer's cottage. The latter formed the setting for 'My Lady of the Chimney Corner' by Alexander Irvine; a deeply-moving true-life love story, which ran to more than fifty editions.

While Irvine's Catholic mother and Protestant father struggled heroically against famine, sectarianism and poverty, a few miles distant, Charlotte Brontë - the author of 'Jane Eyre' - was busy writing her final work, 'Emma', as she enjoyed her nine month long honeymoon in the parish of Killead.

Towering over the historic Antrim Parish Church is a skyscraping embattled tower, the erection of which in the early years of the nineteenth century dramatically redrew the town skyline. With Catholic emancipation and the opening of the first Catholic chapel in Antrim (1820), the historic necessity for mass to be celebrated secretly at open-air refuges was at an end. Three-quarters of the population was Protestant but it was nothing sectarian which drew the attention of the 1830s O.S. Memoir chronicler: "The Sabbath is nowhere in Ireland (outwardly) more strictly observed than here, but it is feared that the public houses are too much frequented on that day by those who come to town from the country to attend worship".

The new century also saw extensive alterations to Antrim Castle. The addition of Clotworthy House (1840) provided an elegant Neo-Tudor coach house and stables complex within the castle grounds. The Market Square entrance to the grounds was enhanced with the addition of a grand barbican gatehouse (1818). Most of the castle walls date from this period also though a unique seventeenth century artillery emplacement survives and has been recently restored.

A superb new Shane's Castle was built (1865) by Charles Lanyon, the famous architect responsible for such other buildings as the Queen's University and Customs House in Belfast. The old 1580 castle of Shane MacBrian O'Neill, however, had been destroyed by fire in 1816. At that time, the architect of London's Regent Street and Regent's Park had been commissioned to swivel Shane's Castle to face south rather than east. Though a new battlemented terrace and exquisite camellia house escaped the fire, work on the first floor of an extension to the castle was brought to a premature end.

Rural and urban districts benefited greatly from the construction of new road and rail communications. Importation of goods and export of farm produce was stimulated. Antrim was the central junction for coaches on the new mail coach road from Belfast bound for Ballymena, Magherafelt or Derry. The Ulster Railway from Belfast arrived in 1848. Soon, Antrim, Randalstown and Toome folk found that they could zoom to the city at a breathtaking twenty miles an hour; twice as fast and half as expensive as road transport. Both the railway and charabancs encouraged

tourism and the growth of local hotels. Nonetheless, railway mania eventually undermined some local industries - the small Antrim brewery in Mill Row (Riverside), for example - by providing better and cheaper products.

At this time, houses in Antrim numbered 382, the other market towns of Crumlin and Randalstown had 100 and 51 respectively, Templepatrick had 30 and Toombridge about 10. In many of these small homes, the people still pursued traditional crafts of spinning and weaving. Merchants from Belfast and Carrickfergus opened offices in Antrim for the purchase of cotton, calico and hosiery. But the days of the domestic cottage industry were under threat.

The distinctive revolution of the nineteenth century was a socio-economic one. The Industrial Revolution injected work and money into the Antrim area, creating a new and important middle class. When the cotton spinning industry was mechanised in Lancashire, Antrim weavers found the competition crippling and switched to the more demanding art of industrial linen weaving.

Flax, an important cash crop for farmers, flourished on rural Antrim's lowlands. The area was soon hailed as Ireland's most extensive bleachgreen, with nearly one half of the adult male population engaged in the manufacture of linen. At Crumlin, Ferguson's mill had begun spinning flax as early as 1812. Down the length of the Sixmilewater valley were mills sporting great water-wheels, some 22 feet in diameter and 6ft broad, which provided the locomotive power behind the area's roaring landscape. Water-wheels sent the power of the river to belt-driven looms and spinning machines. Later, water power was supplemented by steam, the height of modern technology.

The mills were of simple design and bore the stamp of extreme practicality. Former eighteenth century corn, flour and paper-manufacturing mills were converted into linen weaving factories. At Dunadry, the old paper mill founded by William III's court printer, Daniel Blow, switched to linen manufacture.

Heavy or 'medium' yarns were produced at the Cogry Flax Spinning Company's thirty acre complex at Doagh. Accounts of everyday life about Victorian Cogry, Kilbride and Doagh villages are vividly recreated in Florence Mary McDowell's books, 'Other Days Around Me' and 'Roses and Rainbows'.

'Old Bleach Linens' brought international fame to Randalstown's Old Bleach Linen Company. On the site of the ancient iron works, in 1863 the company began a century of manufacturing and bleaching linen. It employed an American turbine and breast wheels operating at a hundred horse-power. In addition, there was a seventy horse-power high pressure engine. Hand-painted woven table damasks originated here. The factory boasted offices in both London and New York.

At Muckamore, the York Street Flax Spinning Company established another great mill complex. It had bought over the country's largest bleachworks from a local linen magnate. A branch railway line from Islandbawn ferried shipments of coal to feed its ravenous steam engines. From 1883 to 1961 the mill played a major role in the local economy. The village community that developed around the mill still survives in the neat rows of terraced homes.

Glenoak mills - the first flour mills in the north of Ireland - built at Crumlin in 1765 and destroyed by fire in 1884 were replaced by the Ulster Woollen Company which manufactured the famous 'Lough Neagh Tweeds'.

Sadly, the days of the textile mills were also unnatural ones: children slaved from six in the morning to six at night, beside pregnant mothers who stood by their looms until natural labour forced them home. Working amid constant and humid clouds of ammonia and graphite, few workers in the 'dark satanic mills' were without a racking cough.

The surging mill-race, which accompanies the Sixmilewater down through the winding Vale of Moylena, has lost little of its power, though the machinery of the noisy beetling mills has long since fallen silent. Today's visitor - whether a naturalist, industrial archaeologist, rambler or simple romantic - can find much to delight in Antrim's picturesque glen.

The new urban prosperity encouraged farmers to bring their produce to town for sale. A corn mill at Riverside in Antrim purchased grain which farmers had dried according to traditional practice: "A fire was lighted against a wall or ditch; branches of trees were placed in a slanting position against the top of the wall or ditch; over these wheat was closely spread, and upon that a layer of grain was spread, which, when it was dried by the heat, was carefully brushed down the straw into a winnowing-sheet, and replaced by a fresh layer of grain," (O.S. Memoir). Rural Antrim at this period was particularly distinguished for its rich harvests of oats, potatoes and flax. Orchards, plantations and hedgerows were numerous.

Southwards from Antrim along the lough shore stretched what was hailed as the Great Wheat Belt of Ulster. These farmers were noted innovators, being the country's first to use threshing machines. The 1793-1815 French and British wars had boosted local grain prices. Deliberate encouragement of tillage helped landowners break down the old and ruinous Scots and Irish Rundale farming practices. (No longer were farms sub-divided according to the number of heirs in a farmer's family.) Their lands were well drained, highly cultivated and efficiently fenced, where corncrakes and lapwings called. However, competition from American grain in the 1870s stimulated a changeover to a livestock-based agricultural economy. Most local smallholdings were amalgamated and turned over to grass.

Weekly market days brought the country to the bustling town. The main street was lined with stalls crowded with old clothes, footwear, crockery, tinware, ironmongery, fruit and gingerbread. Servants and 'hands', both male and female, were obliged to be hired at public street fairs each May and November, all their world wrapped in brown paper parcels carried beneath their arms. Spittle-cum-hand-slapping may conjure up quaint rustic images but the 'hiring ground' was truly a slave market.

Great local horse fairs of the nineteenth century were staged at the Holestone (and Ballyclare). Dealers were attracted from as far away as Scotland, England and Dublin. Around 1840, local farmers established the Antrim Union Farming Society and instituted annual 'cattle shows'. Prizes were awarded for ploughing, digging, crop growing and 'thorough draining'.

Ever since the 1798 uprising, an Act had prohibited public meetings except at the fairs and the loughshore Easter games. Each Easter Monday, young men and women would meet socially at the loughshore for something akin to a romantic sports day. Public recreation being forbidden at all other times led the author of the O.S. Memoir to deduce: "To private meetings, seven-eights of the immorality of the parish may be traced"!

To combat the spread of infection and disease, dispensaries had been established since 1817 at Antrim, Crumlin, Doagh and Randalstown. The Poor Law Union Workhouse in Antrim was established (1843) in the wake of a fierce cholera epidemic. 1051 inmates died in its fever hospital and were interred in the Paupers' graveyard at the rear.

Though famine raged across Ireland during 1845-52, Ulster fatalities generally ran at about only sixteen per cent. Antrim was saved from the worst effects of the famine years, family income generally not being wholly dependent on agricultural labour. With earnings from flax growing, weaving linen or working on the construction of the Ulster Railway from Belfast, rent could still be paid.

Official figures for the three decades following the 1836 population census (which recorded 2,655 citizens in Antrim) reveal a population decline of some 517. It was the beginning of a trend - 1,647 residents in 1881 - that continued until near the end of the century when the 1891 census identified 1,965 inhabitants.

Among Antrim's other notable historic buildings surviving from the nineteenth century are Sir Charles Lanyon's imposing Holywell Hospital (1898), Viscount Massereene's horseshoe-entrance blacksmith's forge (1887), Protestant Hall (1867), Ulster Bank (1865), the former Royal Irish Constabulary barracks in Market Square (1856), High Street's Victorian Gothic church (1853) and the National School which operated in Fountain Street from 1841. For those who could afford it, tuition was also provided by charitable societies, church schools and in the homes of individual teachers.

The revolution that exploded across Mid-Antrim at the start of the twentieth century was essentially agricultural. Whereas, formerly, crop seed had always been scattered by hand, the new century saw seed sown and crops harvested mechanically. Where, once, cutting eight acres of wheat or oats in a day could only be effected by eighty men wielding sickles, now the same task was easily undertaken by a single binding machine and one attendant. An agricultural committee formed to stage ploughing contests and annual carnival 'shows' of horses, cattle, sheep, pigs, poultry and agricultural implements. The field adjacent to the railway station was given to the Antrim Agricultural Society in 1906 as its Show Grounds. It boasted a six hundred seater grandstand, erected at a cost of £1000. The property became a YMCA camp for Great War troops and remains still in military hands.

Both the estates of Shane's Castle and Antrim Castle accommodated thousands of troops during the Great War. In 1922, the historic Shane's Castle was destroyed by arsonists. That same year, during a Grand Ball at Antrim Castle, fire gutted the entire building. The Massereene family was forced to move into their former coach house, Clotworthy House, where, in 1956, the 12th Viscount Massereene passed away. The family seat is now Chilham Castle, Canterbury. Their Antrim estate passed to the citizens of Antrim.

Thereafter, the gaunt ruins of Antrim Castle and its estate were reputed to be haunted by the ghosts of His Lordship and a servant who perished in the castle fire. Following various reports of two white apparitions swooping down from the castle ruins with wailful mourning calls, the local police mounted a 'ghost watch'. The officers were rewarded with a visitation by two large and ghostly-white shapes descending upon them from the charred ruins of the castle: two large, white owls!

Antrim Castle wore its death mask for almost half of the twentieth century before being finally bulldozed. An 1887 hexagonal Italian tower remains, overlooking the restored and now unique seventeenth century Anglo-Dutch water gardens and wooded parkland.

Among the grandchildren of Sam Cody (who emigrated from Antrim to North America in the eighteenth century), was Samuel Franklin Cody: Texan cowboy, bronco-buster, frontiersman, circus sharp-shooter, horse racer, showman and pioneer aviator. When this Indian-fighting, poker-playing son of America's Wild West came to Britain, he invented for the War Office a kite capable of carrying a soldier over enemy positions. It wasn't long before this trail being blazed by S.F. Cody was to lead to Antrim's old Deer Park.

Just a half dozen years after the Wright Brothers made man's first successful flight in a heavier-than-air machine, Harry Ferguson (inventor of the world-famous Ferguson tractor) became the first Briton to build and fly his own aircraft. After a brief trial lift-off at Hillsborough, Ferguson made his first successfully sustained flight from Antrim's Deer Park (April 1910), in his famous 35 h.p. eight cylinder JAP engine aeroplane.

In the same district, just five miles from Antrim town, the Province's first aerodrome - Aldergrove - was constructed in 1917 as a training station for the Royal Flying Corps. Subsequently, Nutts Corner was developed as the Province's civilian airport but, in 1963, transferred to Aldergrove to create Belfast International Airport. Today, it is even possible to hire a private aircraft or helicopter for a bird's eye view of the area. Deserving mention too in this context is Martin Baker Aircraft Ltd. at Langford Lodge, which pioneered the development of the aircraft ejector seat.

The Second World War brought thousands of British, American, Belgian and Dutch army units to the district. Bases established included Ballycraigy, Greenmount, Dunadry, Antrim Castle and Shane's Castle estates. POW camps were created at the Railway Street Showgrounds, beside Antrim railway station and near Toome. Lough Neagh became a vast assembly and training ground for the Allied invasions of Europe and North Africa. Glenn Miller played two concerts at Langford Lodge in August, 1944. Former wartime buildings now house a heritage centre run by the Ulster Aviation Society.

Langford Lodge (Station 597) became the United States Air Force's principal European repair depot, operated by the Lockheed Overseas Corporation. Twenty thousand USAAF servicemen took over the RAF's defence of the Province. Continuous harassment of the enemy was made possible by flying out from this area (and others) combat crew replacements for lost British crews.

Langford Lodge was also the ancestral home of Sir Edward Pakenham, (1779-1815). The Duke of Wellington promoted him to Adjutant-General in the Peninsular war against Napoleon. While commanding the British Army during the 1812-14 American War, Pakenham was killed at the Battle of New Orleans; tradition has it that his heart was buried on the battlefield before his body was brought home.

For much of the first half of the twentieth century, hotel business around Antrim continued to flourish with tourists from home and abroad finding the district convenient for tours of the glens, Antrim coast and the Mountains of Mourne. Most popular were the package holidays for cotton mill workers of Lancashire.

The local linen manufacturing industry survived well into the twentieth century. The great mills at Muckamore and Randalstown continued production within living memory. However, when synthetic fibres undermined the market in the 1950s and 1960s, the old linen mills were forced to close their doors for good. Today, the linen tradition barely survives, though an old factory in Antrim's Riverside is still in daily operation.

Antrim was officially declared a New Town in the 1960s, ripe for industrial development. From a population of 1800, plans were set in motion to attract thousands of new citizens.

A plentiful supply of labour, water and pollution-free atmosphere favoured Antrim as the location for a major man-made fibres manufacturing plant. For the production of nylon and carpet yarns, a labour force of many hundreds was engaged by British Enkalon, a subsidiary of the Akzo Group of companies of Arnhem, Holland. HRH Princess Beatrix, Crown Princess of the Netherlands, officially opened the Enkalon industrial complex in 1963. The factory rapidly expanded and diversified to produce nylon carpet and industrial yarns.

Though the 1970s realised much of the town planners' dreams for education, health, transport, recreation and housing, the crisis that eventually struck down the UK man-made textile industry decimated Antrim's gigantic industrial base in 1982. Smaller and prospering businesses now thrive in the old Enkalon complex and some of the old mills of the district.

The industrial landscape today is characterised by compact business parks and complexes for technological research and development; the thrust is towards the future. A futuristic Technology Park adds a dynamic centre for economic and scientific development.

Superb recreational and social amenities were provided with the opening of the award-winning Antrim Forum. Elsewhere, the area is renowned for championship golf courses, bowling greens, equestrian centres, motor and water sports.

After several centuries as a town with just some three hundred dwellings, Antrim attracted a population of tens of thousands in the closing decades of the twentieth century. The area's strategic easy access to sea and air transport, excellent motorway communications, ultra-modern health, education and recreation facilities, progressive industries and talented citizens holds great promise for the beginning of a new millennium.

Dear Reader

We hope you have enjoyed this book. It is one of a range of illustrated titles which we publish. Other areas currently featured include:–

Strangford Shores   Donegal Highlands
Dundalk & North Louth   Drogheda & the Boyne Valley
Armagh   The Mournes
Belfast   Fermanagh
Cookstown & Mid-Ulster

Also available in our 'Illustrated History & Companion Range' are:-

Ballycastle and the Heart of the Glens   Larne and the Road to the Glens
Coleraine and the Causeway Coast   City of Derry
Hillsborough   Banbridge
Ballymoney   Holywood
Lisburn

We can also supply prints, individually signed by the artist, of the paintings featured in the above titles as well as many other areas of Ireland.

For more details on these superb publications and to view samples of the paintings they contain, you can visit our web site at **www.cottage-publications.com** or alternatively you can contact us as follows:-

Telephone: (028) 9188 8033   Fax: (028) 9188 8063

or write to:-

Cottage Publications
15 Ballyhay Road
Donaghadee, Co. Down
N. Ireland, BT21 0NG

NEVEREVERLAND

WHERE'S MICHAEL?
and many others...

MICHAEL PICKS HIS NOSE

ILLUSTRATIONS

Tim Bywater, Jacqueline Chan, Michael Delmar, Anna Farrell, Rebecca Hartstein, Christian Mirra, Charmaine Ng, Scott Nolan, Kasia Pawlikowski, Diana Thung and Muza Ulazowski

TEXT

Xavier Waterkeyn

NH
NEW HOLLAND

Acknowledgements

Xavier Waterkeyn would like to thank Fiona Schultz and the New Holland team for giving him yet another opportunity to indulge. Thanks to Deleece Cook for all her help too.
He'd also like to extend an extra big thank-you to the twelve talented illustrators who worked on the drawings in this book and produced excellence in record time.

Xavier would like to dedicate this book to every who's ever been called 'eccentric'.
Without eccentric people the world would be an unliveably boring place.

Shira Bentley would like to thank Xavier Waterkeyn and New Holland Publishing for the opportunity to be involved in such a fun and unique project.

Tim Bywater would like to thank his Nan, The Mars Volta and Jesus.

Jacqueline Chan would like to thank Xavier Waterkeyn and New Holland and dedicates her drawing to everyone who loves Christmas.

Michael Delmar would really just like to thank Xavier and New Holland for the opportunity to share in the project. Thank you immensely.

Anna Farrell would like to give her very special thanks to everyone frustrated by her arty, erratic moods and intense secrecy during this project, to Ben and Karl for their techological wisdom, to Em, Mills and Claire B for undying support and to Chook who never strays over the line.

Rebecca Harstein thanks her mum and dad for encouraging her do an art degree instead of a real degree, and actually all her relatives for pretending to like the millions of silly drawings she did. Also the College of Fine Arts, for lending her computer time and scanner time, and not complaining when she returned tablets after 3 days instead of 3 hours. And Zacc, for being there.

Christian Mirra would like to thank Georgia Taperell and Xavier Waterkeyn for giving him the opportunity to work on this book. He'd like to dedicate his work to Sergio D'Argenio and Antonio Cella because they are such a great team to make comics with.

Charmaine Ng would like to thank her family and friends for their unfaltering love and support (especially staying up with me at ungodly hours) and Xavier for creating this awesome project!

Scott Nolan would like to thank his girlfriend Kara and her family the Baird's for all the help and support as well as Xavier and New Holland for giving him this opportunity. He dedicates his work to his family, Annette, Gary and Brock.

Diana Thung would like to thank her mother for letting her do art.

Muza Ulazowski thanks the support and encouragement of her long-suffering husband Arkady who cheerfully puts up with her constantly disappearing behind a computer, and to her lovely girls Sasha and Lara for their unfailing belief in her ability.

Transcript of Exposé Special – The 'Real' Michael Jackson originally aired on Channel 69 Friday, June 25 2010.

MONTAGE OF ARCHIVAL CLIPS OF MICHAEL JACKSON – PERFORMING, BEING CHASED BY PAPARAZZI, KISSING LISA-MARIE, KISSING HIS CHILDREN, KISSING OTHER PEOPLE'S CHILDREN, KISSING BUBBLES THE CHIMP

VO: Tonight on Exposé. Amid the controversy, the hysteria and the melodrama that still surrounds Michael Jackson's untimely death there remains the mystery of his life. Just who was this enigmatic figure whose every movement was fodder for both fans and critics alike? Saint? Sinner? Diva or Demon? In this Exposé special investigative correspondent Lech Moocher uncovers some startling new facts of the life of the late King of Pop.

INT. STUDIO L/S L.M. ON CHAIR
CUT TO INT. STUDIO MCU L.M. – L.M. TO CAMERA

LECH MOOCHER: Good evening and thank you for joining us. It's one year ago today that the world was shocked to hear of the death of Michael Joseph Jackson.

CUT TO ARCHIVE FOOTAGE OF HYSTERICAL MOURNING FANS

HMF 1: Oh my God! Oh my God! He was s-s-s-so beautiful. S-s-s-so s-s-s-special!
HMF 2: He was my worrrrlllllddd!!!!

CUT TO INT. STUDIO MCU L.M. – L.M. TO CAMERA

LM: And although his death continues to be plagued with unanswered, or rather unsatisfactorily answered questions …

CUT TO MONTAGE OF ARCHIVE FOOTAGE FROM VARIOUS NEWS SOURCES OF MJ AMBULANCE

CUT TO INT. STUDIO MCU L.M. – L.M. TO CAMERA

LM: … this state of affairs is no different to what was, for Michael Jackson at least, normal life.

CUT TO ARCHIVE FOOTAGE OF M.J. INTERVIEW

MJ: Look. I've only had two rhinoplasties and a cleft put in my chin to help me with my singing. Everything else is just growing up, makeup, lighting and vitiligo. All these stories about extensive plastic surgery and eye-liner tattoos are crazy. I don't know where people get these ideas from.

CUT TO ARCHIVE FOOTAGE OF ANOTHER M.J. INTERVIEW

MJ: No. No. NO! I do not sleep in an enriched oxygen bubble. I do not own the bones of the Elephant Man and just because Bubbles knows how to clean toilets and keep my room tidy does not mean that he's a domestic slave who works for peanuts. I don't know where people get these ideas from.

CUT TO ARCHIVE FOOTAGE OF INTERVIEW WITH LA TOYA JACKSON

LTJ: The only reason that you never see Michael and me in the same photograph is that we live so far apart. We are NOT the same person. I am not my brother in drag. That's just stupid. I don't know where people get these ideas from.

CUT TO INT. STUDIO MCU L.M. – L.M. TO CAMERA

L.M.: But tonight we may just be able to quash some of these and some other even more outrageous rumors once and for all. While at the same time we will reveal a host of previously unknown facts of the life of the late King of Pop. More about that, after the break.

LM: In the confusion, media frenzy, tacky commercial exploitation of Michael Jackson's memory and free-for-all grab that followed Jackson's death, crazed fans stormed Neverland and raided the compound taking advantage of a once-in-a-lifetime opportunity to snatch souvenirs, memorabilia and relics. If you've never heard this story before it's because the Jackson Estate quashed it. In fact, the incredible stories that actually got out pale, like so many other things Jackson, compared with the stories that were successfully suppressed - until now. But just what are these stories and what evidence do we have for them? Well, one fan, who has chosen to remain anonymous, found a secret stash of photos dating back decades. They reveal events in Jackson's life that only serve to highlight the frenetic media circus and chaos that seemed to follow Jackson wherever he went.

We have, as yet, no way of knowing who actually took these pictures or what Jackson paid so that they would never see the light of day but here, now, and exclusive to Exposé we now bring them to you in the interest of public disclosure. The pictures uniformly show Jackson, his friends and family in situations far from the sanitized, doctored, manipulated and flattering images that celebrities usually approve for publication. These then are the images (and the arrests!) that Michael Jackson didn't want you to see.

Photographic experts have yet to determine the origin or authenticity of these pictures but we feel that the public has a right to see these pictures and judge for themselves. Michael Jackson himself is often difficult to find, and, curiously, analysis reveals that there are certain objects and themes that are common to all of them. For your reference the objects in question that you can find in each picture panel are:

ADD ON-SCREEN GRAPHIC SUPERIMPOSITION

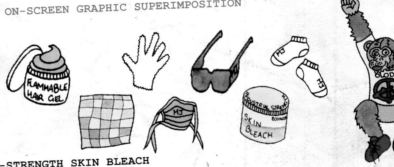

BUBBLES THE CHIMP
A BLANKET
A DIAMOND-STUDDED GLOVE
A PAIR OF MONOGRAMMED WHITE SOCKS
A PAIR OF MONOGRAMMED DARK GLASSES
A MONOGRAMMED SURGICAL MASK
A JAR OF HAIR GEL - EXTRA FLAMMABLE
A JAR OF GIANT ECONOMY-SIZE INDUSTRIAL-STRENGTH SKIN BLEACH

REMOVE ON-SCREEN GRAPHIC SUPERIMPOSITION

The pictures themselves may require some explanation. The image to the right of your screen shows MJ as depicted in the pictures

① This picture allegedly shows what seems to be a food fight breaking out between the Jacksons and the Osmonds on the set of the Ed Sullivan Show some time in early February 1970. Since there is no record of such a show ever being recorded we can only conclude that it was cancelled on account of Jackson's arrest for assault and the release of signature Jackson 5 song 'ABC' then had to occur on American Bandstand later that month.

② During the taping of a commercial for Schlepsi Cola in October 1983 things went horribly wrong. Jackson is arrested for suspected arson. Several months later Jackson tries with another cola company, and on 27 January 1984 things went horribly wrong - again.

③ Apparently inspired by the horrors of the commercial filming incidents, Jackson writes one of his best known songs and experiments with a theme park based on the song that Jackson planned to open in January 1984. Jackson is arrested for building code violations, and it is ordered to be torn down. The park is never opened and all records of it erased - except for this single image.

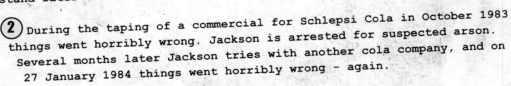

(4) April 1984. After the second cola disaster Jackson is treated for burns and decides that since he's going to go under the knife anyway, he will take advantage of one of Saint Narcissus Hospital's 'three for the price of two' rhytidectomy specials. He is arrested shortly after on suspicion of causing willful bodily harm *to himself.*

(5) Having suffered for his art and feeling guilty that Bob Geldof thought of it first, Jackson is moved to empathize for those who are suffering just for being alive and records a famine relief charity song with a cast of dozens in November 1984. With producers having forgotten to check the singer's egos at the door, the recording session is a failure and Jackson is forced to re-record the song with a catchier title and more syrupy lyrics on 27 January 1985. Jackson is later arrested for inducing diabetic comas in susceptible individuals who have listened to the song.

(6) Three months into his marriage to Lisa-Marie Presley, Jackson holds a sleepover party for over a hundred of his best friends on 10 August 1994. Presley was, of course, invited. Jackson is arrested for running a child-care facility without a license.

(7) Haunted by allegations of varying misconducts Jackson pens an angst-ridden song about persecution and intolerance. During the filming of the clip in the slums of Salvador, Brazil in June 1995 authorities arrest Jackson for patronizing the third world. Jackson rewrites lyrics and song title only to be accused of anti-Semitism back home, requiring more re-writes. Delays mean the song isn't released until April Fools Day 1996.

(8) Post-ceremony party of the Empty V Awards on 7 September 1995. Jackson would be arrested later that night for 'inappropriate handling of hors-d'oeuvres.'

(9) Traumatized by his numerous arrests Jackson retreats into the fantasy world of Christmas only to be arrested again on the evening of 24 December 1995 on charges of 'inciting reindeer to assume humiliating positions'.

(10) Unable to find release from the pressures of fame and tangles with the American legal system, Jackson seeks refuge in consumerism and in March 2005 buys several million dollars' worth of trash Versace ornaments and soft furnishings at Billie's Jean Emporium only to be arrested for 'gross violations of local statutes of good taste.'

(11) In an effort to pay his ever-mounting legal debts Jackson holds a foreclosure party at Neverland in May 2008. Later that day he will be arrested by the Santa Barbara sheriffs department, for impersonating a police officer while riding his FLHPEI model Harley Davidson rear-wheel drive, fuel-injected, Big Twin 2-cylinder engine, touring motorcycle complete with flashing lights and annoyingly load siren!

(12) Later a further image would come to light. On 29 July 2009 the dress rehearsal for Jackson's funeral would become the latest in a long line of fiascos as fans storm Forest Lawn Memorial Park. We believe that because Jackson was now firmly convinced that authorities were out to get him with ever more ridiculous and unsubstantiated allegations, and because no amount of adulation or shopping could save him, Michael Jackson decided to use his 'connections' to fake his own death. The evidence is there, if you look hard enough for it.

LM: Here then are the pictures themselves. There's a checklist at the end of this show as well to help you find all the hidden objects.

This is Lech Moocher, and you're watching Exposé. We'll be right back with you after the break.

CUT TO COMMERCIAL

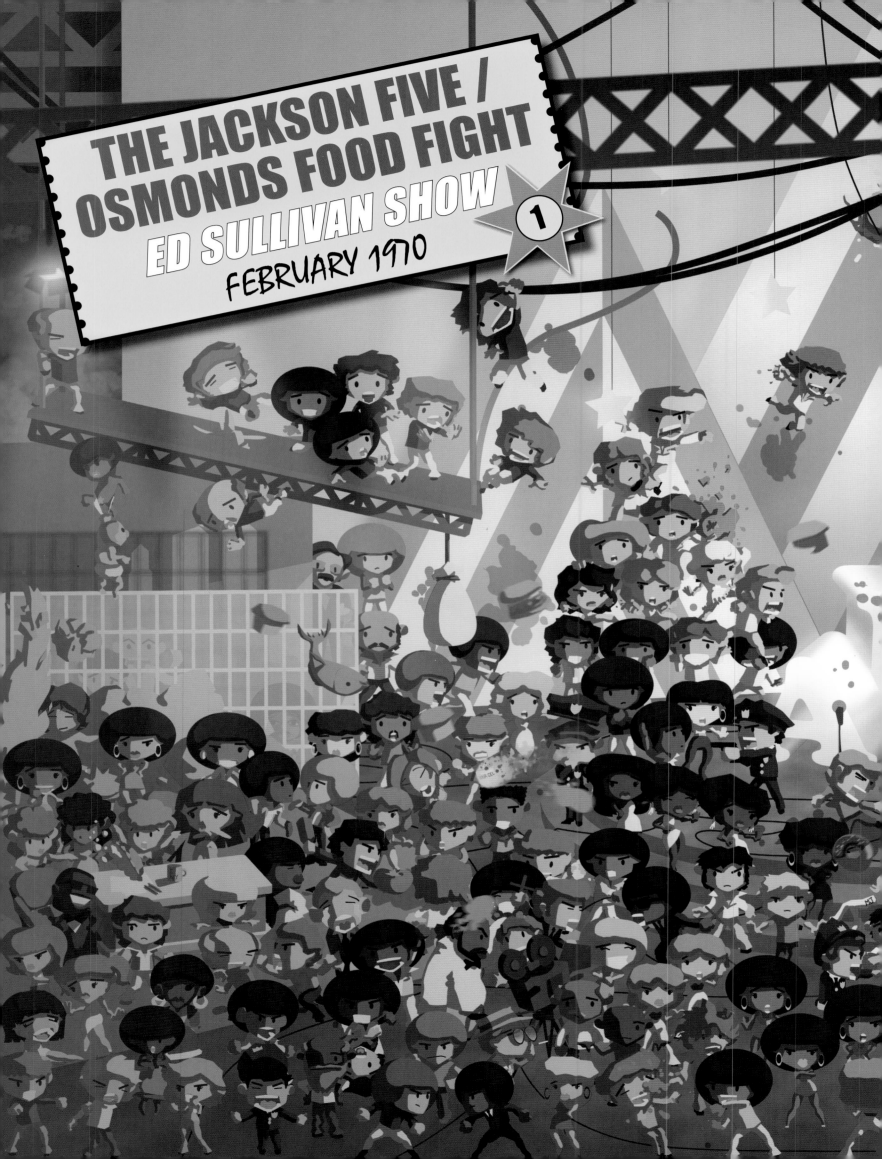

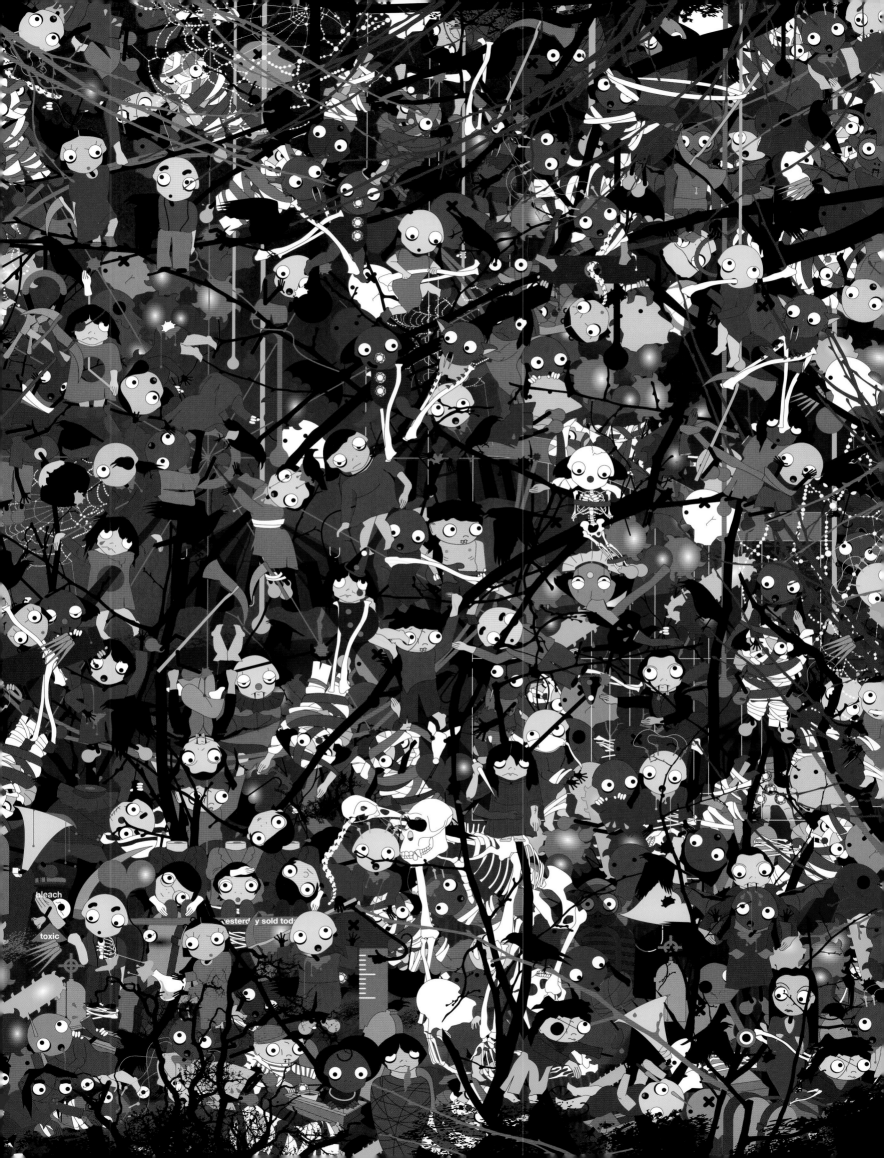

A VERY MICHAEL CHRISTMAS

9 NEVERLAND RANCH

DECEMBER 1995

Take a dangling photo with Santa

OBJECTS OF INTEREST TO THE DISCERNING EXAMINER:

The Jackson / Osmond Food Fight – February 1970

- ☐ Joe Jackson cashing in
- ☐ Isaac Hayes pulling his weight
- ☐ Aretha Franklin (kind of just standing there being a natural woman)
- ☐ Kool and the Gang being way too cool for the gang
- ☐ Ed Sullivan having a tantrum
- ☐ Baby Janet having a diaper malfunction with Justin Timberlake's elder cousin Steve
- ☐ Two sneaky Afro Ninjas hiding in the shadows
- ☐ Smiley Stevie Wonder
- ☐ Partridge Family flying in for some action
- ☐ Bruce Lee putting up a fight for the Jackson 5
- ☐ Jim Morrison spacing out in the bushes
- ☐ Hunter S. Thompson getting new ideas

Michael's Inferno – October 1983

- ☐ Joe Jackson
- ☐ Macaulay Caulkin doing his best impersonation of 'The Scream' by Edvard Munch
- ☐ Salvador Dali's clocks melting in the heat
- ☐ Marcel Duchamp's 'Fountain' signed as R. Mutt
- ☐ A Not-So-Smooth Criminal
- ☐ An exploding mirror ball
- ☐ A burning merry-go-round
- ☐ A demon racing across the ceiling
- ☐ A pot of strawberry jam, bubbling away in the heat
- ☐ A smiley button
- ☐ A slick of blood on the floor
- ☐ 8 butterflies

Thrillerland – January 1984

- ☐ 8 hidden Grammy Awards
- ☐ Elizabeth Taylor as the Bride of Frankenstein
- ☐ The shower scene from Psycho
- ☐ Two crows roosting in eye sockets
- ☐ The head of Frankenstein's Monster
- ☐ A battle with Death
- ☐ A headless horseman
- ☐ A two-headed zombie
- ☐ Two acid throwers
- ☐ A set of twins
- ☐ A headless clown
- ☐ The Beatles

Michael Goes the Plastic – April 1984

- ☐ Vat of liposucked celebrity fat
- ☐ Two of Bin Laden's Posse detonating a bomb in a delivery van of spare body parts
- ☐ Mr Potato Head selling items from his Fall Celebrity Disguise Collection

- ☐ Buffalo Bill from 'The Silence of the Lambs' finding a good swatch of discarded human skin
- ☐ Eskimo using Nemo the Clownfish as bait
- ☐ 7 patients wrapped-up to the point of mummyhood
- ☐ Man being accidently decapitated by helicopter (lucky he's near a hospital)
- ☐ 258 augmented, modified or 'enhanced' breasts
- ☐ 2 natural breasts
- ☐ Donut cop
- ☐ Piñata full of prescription candy
- ☐ Bag of givaway promotional dolls, one free with every procedure, collect all 25!

The World is Us – November 1984

- ☐ Willie Nelson getting his pigtails pulled by a certain person who shall remain nameless
- ☐ Billie Joel getting his fingers slammed in a piano
- ☐ Roadie with an audio cable going in one ear and out the other
- ☐ Ozzy Osbourne throwing up
- ☐ Flying Banana
- ☐ Watusi Dancer
- ☐ Steve Perry's agent screaming on the hotline at him wondering why he hasn't shown up yet.
- ☐ Fan girl lifting her shirt to show off her underwear
- ☐ Pointer Sisters pointing to each other
- ☐ Light technician auditioning for a part in a Tarot deck
- ☐ Tina Turner getting a wig fitted from the Mr Potato Head collection
- ☐ Man about to get electrocuted with his urine

Neverland Sleepover – August 1994

- ☐ Kid waking up to discover a kid lying on top of him has urinated on him in his sleep
- ☐ Stuffed, bleached flying pig
- ☐ Monogrammed mutant pig
- ☐ Unmonogrammed crocodile
- ☐ Unmonogrammed, giant, economy-sized Grammy Award (saves the planet by using fewer resources for the same amount of laudation)
- ☐ Hamburger
- ☐ Julian Lennon earning a few bucks standing-in for his father
- ☐ Boy sticking chewing gum into Lisa-Marie's hair
- ☐ Three arrows
- ☐ 238, 967 feathers
- ☐ Original Thriller album cover
- ☐ Cowboy hat
- ☐ Box of two-toned chocolates

They Don't Care About Me - June 1995

- [ ] A leopard
- [ ] A Carmen Miranda fan wearing a fruit headdress
- [ ] Soccerplayers
- [ ] A thong bikini
- [ ] 2 toucans
- [ ] 12 cameras
- [ ] 2 bras
- [ ] 22 moustaches
- [ ] 3 non-Bubbles monkeys (who's a chimp, anyway)
- [ ] 2 film reels in the process of getting misplaced
- [ ] 5 sets of camera lights
- [ ] A hand giving the peace sign

The Empty V Awards - September 1995

- [ ] A penguin that's escaped from Michael's collection of two-toned animals
- [ ] Janet Jackson rehearsing a future wardrobe malfunction
- [ ] Whitney Houston testing out some icing sugar
- [ ] Scary Spice wearing a 'Whose Your Daddy?' shirt
- [ ] Eddie Murphy wearing a t-shit denying responsibility for fathering Scary Spice's daughter
- [ ] A tray of suspicious brownies
- [ ] 5 multi-colored ninjas stealing Cher's wigs
- [ ] Paris Hilton making a video
- [ ] 3 drunken swans dealing with the trauma of seeing Bjork's dress
- [ ] A tooth from the fight between Liam and Noel Gallagher from Oasis
- [ ] 3 Chihuahuas doing what Chihuahuas do
- [ ] Mariah Carey and her entourage of pink toilet rolls

A Very Michael Christmas - December 2002

- [ ] Debbie Rowe patting her pregnant belly
- [ ] Tim Allen unable to let his Santa persona go
- [ ] Three zombie refugees a certain video
- [ ] Two veiled children whose identities shall remain mysteries
- [ ] A child feeding a bauble to another child
- [ ] Three pairs of kids dueling with candy canes
- [ ] A boy with a present smashed over his head and around his neck
- [ ] A politically correct black Santa Claus
- [ ] Four moon-walking reindeer
- [ ] A kid roasting nose-shaped marshmallows
- [ ] Macaulay sulkin'
- [ ] Janet acclimatizing her breast to exposure (again)

Michael Goes Shopping - March 2005

- [ ] Marcel Marceau, Lionel Ritchie and Woody Allen
- [ ] Woman dressed in one of Jean-Charles de Castelbajac's catwalk collection featuring Michael Jackson's head
- [ ] Bust of a unicorn head
- [ ] Tacky King of Pop Crown
- [ ] Pair of full-length retro 70's purple boots
- [ ] Life-size Saddam Hussein doll
- [ ] OJ Simspon orange juice extractor
- [ ] Anna-Nichole Smilh inflato-doll, partially deflated with a 'Reduced to Clear' sign on it
- [ ] Vampire Jack-in-the-box
- [ ] Elephant Man Genuine Reproduction Skeleton
- [ ] Man in the Mirror

Nevereverland - May 2008

- [ ] The clock showing the official time of Michael's death
- [ ] 2 bulldogs
- [ ] The Naked cowboy chasing his horse
- [ ] Brook Sheilds in a blue lagoon
- [ ] Janet malfunctioning again with the help of an elephant
- [ ] Diana Ross giving Elizabeth Taylor a push
- [ ] A bald eagle demonstrating why eagles go bald
- [ ] A hippopotamus eating a camera
- [ ] Zebra relieving himself
- [ ] One very kinky fairy
- [ ] Lisa-Marie in a pair of blue suede shoes
- [ ] Bubble's girlfriend

The Funeral Rehearsal- July 2009

- [ ] 5 hidden ninjas
- [ ] 5 bodyguards inspired on MJ's top hits (Bad, Thriller, Black or White, Billie Jean and Beat it).
- [ ] A suspicious-looking purple dinosaur
- [ ] A familiar-looking large bird
- [ ] A policeman sword fighting with a reporter
- [ ] A fireman shooting water on to a lighter
- [ ] A SWAT soldier getting killed by the flash of a camera
- [ ] 4 members of the National Rifle Association finding and excuse to use their guns
- [ ] 10 limousines
- [ ] 7 helicopters
- [ ] 8 parachutes
- [ ] Gladys Knight no doubt wishing she was on a midnight train to Georgia

Biographies

Xavier Waterkeyn did a variety of dead end-jobs ranging from chicken-stuffer to manager of a psychic centre before finding his true calling as a writer and general, all-round, creative whizz. He's currently working on about half a dozen books at once. He also runs his own manuscript assessment service and literary agency Flying Pigs: xavier@flyingpigs.com.au.

Shira Bentley has been Printmaking at Sydney's COFA for three years. She works with a variety of styles and themes and is inspired by art, music, travel and, in this case, Michael Jackson. [They Don't Care About Me]

Tim Bywater lives in Sydney and works as a freelance illustrator, comic colourist, logo designer and animator. He likes line work, patterns, the effective use of space and subdued colors. He works both traditionally with inks and washes and digitally using Photoshop and Illustrator and likes to animate using Flash. You can see more of his work at www.timbywater.com. [The World is Us]

Jacqueline Chan used to be a boring engineer before taking the leap to becoming a designer. Whimsical and surreal things always inspire her, as life would be boring if everything were logical. [A Very Michael Christmas]

Michael Delmar has recently completed his Bachelor of Fine Arts at the College of Fine Arts Sydney and is now engaged in a Masters of Graphic Design at that very same institution. He's currently paying the bills with some casual design and illustration work examples of which you can see at michaeladelmar.blogspot.com [The Jackson/Osmond Food Fight]

Anna Farrell has been sketching since she could hold a crayon and has been getting commissions since her early teens. Her usual weapons of choice are the humble pencil and fine point black pen, watercolours and inks. See the products of her febrile imagination at: www.eugenethechicken.com [Michael's Inferno]

When **Rebecca Harstein** was young she wanted to be a unicorn, but failing in that she drew pictures of unicorns on everything and ended up being an artist instead. Halfway through a degree at the College of Fine Arts NSW, she's participated in the Headspace exhibition 2006 at the National Portrait Gallery in Canberra and the Chalk Urban Art festival. See more of her work at: www.wix.com/foxinshocks/rebecca-hartstein [Neverland Sleepover]

Christian Mirra is a dangerous international terrorist who achieved social respectability by converting bombs into comic books. He is Italian and lives in Spain and he's still convinced he is converting comic books into bombs. You can see some of his conversions at www.christianmirra.com. [The Funeral Rehearsal]

Charmaine Ng is a happy drunk who believes she lives in a Jean-Pierre Jeunet movie; she spends her days collecting antique junk, taking photos and singing Bohemian Rhapsody in her sleep. She's currently under the process of selling her blood sweat and soul to completing her design degree, striving to bring more whimsical and surreal forms into the world. [Michael Goes Shopping]

Upon completion of a 4-year final double degree in Graphic Design and Visual effects from Charles Sturt University, **Scott Nolan** finally has the piece of paper that proves that he can draw. He's worked in the visual design industry since 2007. See more of his work at: www.scottnolan.com.au [Michael Goes the Plastic]

Kasia Pawlikowski has her own business, zirka&wolf – a Melbourne based visual communication studio specializing in branding and publication design for the cultural sector. Collaboration, experimentation and community contribution are integral to the studio's approach. You can see more of her work at www.zirkawolf.com. [Thrillerland]

Diana Thung was born in Jakarta, Indonesia and later moved to Singapore where she lived for thirteen years before relocating to Sydney. She wants to draw till the day she croaks. Being young, we hope that's a long time coming, but before she does, and maybe even after you can see more of her work at dianathung.com [Empty V Awards]

With her girls now grown up and pursuing their own dreams, **Muza Ulazowski**, for her retirement, decided to resurrect her own career by enrolling fulltime at college to unravel the complexities of the computer world. With a second graphic design diploma now successfully under her belt, she has enthusiastically embarked on an illustrating career. Her work can be viewed at www.muzadesigns.com.au. [Neverland & Michael Picks His Nose]

First published in Australia in 2010 by
New Holland Publishers (Australia) Pty Ltd
Sydney • Auckland • London • Cape Town

1/66 Gibbes Street Chatswood NSW 2067 Australia
218 Lake Road Northcote Auckland New Zealand
86 Edgware Road London W2 2EA United Kingdom
80 McKenzie Street Cape Town 8001 South Africa

Copyright © 2010 New Holland Publishers (Australia) Pty Ltd
Illustrations © individual illustrators

A record of this book is held at the National Library of Australia

ISBN 9781741109757

Publisher: Fiona Schultz
Publishing Manager: Liane Clarke
Designer: Amanda Tarlau
Front cover: Muza Ulazowski   Back cover: Christian Mirra
Production Manager: Olga Dementiev
Printer: Toppan Leefung Printing Limited (China)

10 9 8 7 6 5 4 3 2 1

THIS WAS IT!